THE LIVES OF ALICE POTHRON

ONE WOMAN'S ESCAPE TO FREEDOM

Jenny Harrison

with Evelyne Pothron

Published by:
Lamplighter Press

Check out other titles by this author at:
http://www.jennyharrison.co.nz

Editing, cover design & layout by Bev Robitai
www.thebookcoach.weebly.com

Front cover photo: Alice Pothron, German soldiers
marching into Paris.
Back cover: Emile Pothron with Evelyne.

ACKNOWLEDGEMENTS

My thanks go to Evelyne Pothron for asking me to write this amazing story and giving me whatever information I needed to complete the task. Thanks also to:

- members of my writing group, the Mairangi Writers' Group in Auckland, New Zealand, for all their help and encouragement. Vicky, Barbara, Jean, Evan, Rodney, Maureen, Pam, Peter, Bev, Gabrielle, Erin and Kay. Special thanks to Vicky. Her final edit of this book was invaluable.
- Renée Baecke and Emilienne Person-Perros of Paron for added information.
- Elizabeth and Patrick Negri of Orewa, New Zealand, who spent long hours correcting my flawed (non-existent?) French and for this I can only say: Merci, mes amis.
- Bev Robitai for her superb work in the formatting and layout of this book. Without her expertise, enthusiasm and patience it would be resting in a bottom drawer.
- Pierre Glaizal of Paron has been an exceptional and unexpected friend who has enthusiastically espoused the cause and has spent time digging up information I couldn't possibly have found. Merci beaucoup, Pierre.
- Finally, thanks to Howard, my husband who picks up the pieces as quickly as I drop them.

I have had expert help and read a great many good books on the subject (see the bibliography) but mistakes are inevitable and for them I apologize.

Conversations have had to be deduced from the personalities and their reactions to circumstances.

To protect privacy, some names have been changed and names given to those people who needed to remain anonymous for their own safety and the safety of their family, friends and others who worked for the freedom of France in a dangerous time.

PREFACE

The truth is too precious to become
the slave of fashion.

— Margaret Thatcher

It was a strange encounter.

A blazingly hot day in September 2009 on board a cruise liner in mid-Pacific. There had been a tsunami somewhere and a bomb blast or two in places we had never heard of and were not likely to visit. People had died and babies born while we were cocooned in a make-believe world of luxury.

We were having morning coffee with new-found friends somewhere between Hawaii and Tahiti with the rush of navy-blue Pacific water under the bow and the sun hanging over us like a bronze medallion on a veteran's uniform.

"I've been looking for a writer for years," she said.

Quintessential American in manner but elegant in the way of European women, Evelyne Pothron had a story to tell and I wanted to write it.

Once before I had said an enthusiastic 'yes' when asked to write someone's story **(Debbie's Story)**. Truth to tell I hadn't known then what I was letting myself in for. This time I was only slightly better informed. My instinctive 'yes' to Evelyne has led me on a journey of discovery, not only into the lives of her parents, Alice and Emile Pothron, but also the times in which they lived and the turmoil into which they inadvertently sailed.

Evelyne told me her parents had been born in France but had met in New York where they fell in love and married in 1928. On a return trip to France in 1938, with the Second World War looming, they faced their greatest challenge. This is a heroic tale of an innocent young couple caught up in the German invasion of France in 1940, separated by cruel events, each suffering their own kind of purgatory.

The story their daughter had to tell did not sit well with the hedonistic luxury of a cruise liner. On board the *Star Princess* our fantasy world was in stark contrast to the events experienced by Evelyne's parents and, in particular, her mother. The light cast by the glittering sea seemed to mock the dark deeds perpetrated under German rule. The food we ate would only have been dreamed of by Alice and Emile and others in France during the Second World War. I was aware of the irony. On the one side was the colorful and carefree luxury of a cruise liner and on the other the black deeds of 1940.

Evelyne kindly allowed me to read the story as she had gathered it from her parents when she was a teenager. There were gaps, of course, and fading memory has played its usual tricks. These events occurred more than seventy years ago and those who survived this particular and horrific experience, and who could sort the wheat from the chaff, are long gone. We have only a short memoir of the events and it has been necessary to extrapolate the vague and sometimes conflicting memories and turn them into a coherent story. It was sometimes necessary to imagine, on the basis of history and personality, how the protagonists would have acted and reacted. Having "lived" with the characters for nearly three years, I believe I have got as close to what happened as is possible, given the years that have passed.

In the Author's Note of David Howarth's book **Escape Alone** (Wm Collins, Glasgow, 1960) he says: "Some minor events are a matter of deduction, but none of it is imaginary." I can only reiterate that statement and say that, as far as I am aware, I have deduced but not imagined.

Written history is only one version of the truth. The version lived by people who struggled with fear, hunger, guilt and hopelessness is very different from that of dull dusty history books. This, therefore, is not a historical treatise but the story of two ordinary young people caught up in events not of their choosing and their experiences under the Nazi regime. It is how it was remembered many years after the events by, among others, their daughter.

Not only is this a love story, but it is a devoted daughter's way of honoring her parents and ensuring that they and their story live forever.

Alice & Emile Pothron

CHAPTER 1

Normandie compels because of her exemplary design,
unparalleled luxe and extraordinary chic,
quintessential and incomparable."
- John Maxtone-Graham

Pier 88, New York. A sunny day in July 1938.
Emile and Alice Pothron boarded the elegant cruise
liner *SS Normandie* for a well-earned vacation in
France. They were about to spend five days on the
most beautiful ship in the world followed by a short
holiday in the land of their birth.

It was to become the vacation from hell.

Emile and Alice could not have been aware of the
political instability and turbulence into which they
were sailing. Nor could they have foreseen the horror
of what was to occur.

News of the rise of Nazism in Germany and
Europe's coming tribulations had not been widely
covered by the American media. Or, if it had, the
Pothrons were not aware of it. Varian Fry, a well-
known and respected journalist who later rescued
many refugees from occupied France and became
known as America's Oskar Schindler, had written
extensively in the *New York Times* about the threat to
civilization in Europe and Hitler's planned
extermination of Jews.

No one took him seriously.

Alice and Emile knew little or nothing of this. In
1938 there was no Internet and no television and so
news travelled slowly. Or perhaps they were

insulated by their lifestyles; Emile, a hairstylist to the rich and famous, and Alice, a dress designer whose busy life left little room for international affairs.

American interest in Europe had waned after the successful conclusion of the First World War. When Hitler began his bluster and threats as early as 1933, America nervously pulled its robes around its shoulders and looked the other way, leaving the Continent to ferment alone. It is not surprising that Americans did not know, did not want to know, or perhaps did not care what was happening in Europe although many, like Varian Fry, prophetically wrote that serious trouble was brewing, which would engulf the world.

Americans found the boxers, Joe Louis and Max Schmeling, far more interesting than what was going on in Europe. The title fight was held on Wednesday 22 June 1938 in Yankee Stadium, New York, where "our" Joe soundly trounced the German in the first round. Just as exciting was aviator Howard Hughes' circumnavigation of the globe. On Sunday 10 July 1938, he completed the voyage in ninety-one hours, beating the old record by more than four hours.

After the Great Depression, American confidence was, finally, on the rise.

The *SS Normandie* was ready to sail. On board Alice and Emile watched the massive hawsers slipping into the bay, sliding through the water until they were dragged on board, still dripping with kelp that hung like Spanish moss. The last of the streamers and confetti had settled on the decks leaving sodden trails to tangle unwary shoes. The final strains of *Auld Lang Syne* echoed over Pier 88 as the musicians packed away trombones, triangles and drums and prepared to go on to their next appointment. The sun began to slip behind the battlements of New York City and tugs churned the fetid water, nursing the curved bow of the great cruise liner past the Statue of Liberty and out into the Atlantic.

The *Normandie* gave a final three-note whistle from her forward stack and then they were gone.

The SS Normandie leaving New York

The north Atlantic is an unfriendly ocean, demanding and voracious. For most of the year it is cold, rough and foggy. While it was only a five-day crossing from New York to Le Havre in France, passengers would be subjected to boredom, seasickness or plain terror if the unruly Atlantic tested their resolve.

Members of the crew were acutely aware of the ocean's unsettling nature and had arranged musical entertainment, films, games and other amusements to distract the passengers. Quoits, tennis and three-legged races were the order of the day, although it is hard to imagine a sophisticate like Alice Pothron indulging in deck games.

One of the most entertaining, if informal, pastimes was 'people spotting' and an eager-eyed Alice recognized a number of famous faces among the first-class passengers. For many celebrities it was *de rigueur* to travel and be seen on the *SS Normandie*. Hollywood stars like Greta Garbo, Cary Grant, George Raft, Marlene Dietrich, Fred Astaire, and the notorious dancer Josephine Baker had, at one time or another, been onboard. Writers such as P G Wodehouse, Noël Coward, Ernest Hemingway and Irving Berlin had also been passengers on the luxury French cruise liner.

The *Normandie* was a ship of superlatives; enormous and, without doubt, the most glamorous and elegant ship ever built, bringing French chic and Art Deco luxury to the ocean. Among its many luxuries it had a magnificent dining room, the first air conditioned public room on any ship. Lit by twelve tall pillars of Lalique glass and chandeliers at each end, it had earned *SS Normandie* the name 'Ship of Light'.

In spite of the luxury and speed she was, surprisingly, not particularly popular and averaged an occupancy rate of only forty-nine per cent, making her unprofitable in the long-term. Obviously her first class passengers had no complaints but the tourist-class suffered pokey cabins with bunk beds and shared bathrooms at the end of each passage.

Alice did not fancy walking down the corridor in a bathrobe clutching her toilet bag, so she was delighted when Emile insisted on a first-class cabin with an en-suite bathroom. Alice was perfectly satisfied and determined to revel in the art of comfort for five bliss-filled days.

Travelling by ship was a costly affair in more than the price of the ticket. Certain mores had to be acknowledged and one was a strict dress code. The five-day trip required at least three costume changes a day. Alice was well-prepared. As a professional designer and dressmaker she had made herself a few glamorous evening gowns in the latest New York fashion. In her trunks were day-dresses with padded shoulders and cinched waistlines, coats, clunky-heeled shoes, gloves and hats. She had also secreted a few dozen pairs of the new artificial silk stockings. She was ready to impress.

Another expense had been their pet dog, Skippy. He was housed in the kennels inside the third and dummy funnel of the *Normandie* where the air conditioning units were also located. The kennels opened onto a special doggie promenade that gave Alice the opportunity to exercise and play with her pet. Skippy had been with them from the start; a present from Jacques Laffont, Emile's best friend and partner in their hairstyling business in San Francisco.

Also on board were Alice's aunt and uncle, Louise Fromont and Jules Duxin. Alice would have preferred to visit France without them but it had been out of her hands. Louise had gushed enthusiastically when Emile revealed his plans to visit France. Next thing they knew, Louise had booked a cabin and it looked as if their vacation was about to be a shared one.

Dinner onboard was a glamorous and enjoyable affair, even though they had to share a table with Louise and Jules. Light from the tall pillars cast a symphony of color over the guests. The gold and red-marble bas-relief on the walls absorbed and muted the conversations. White-robed waiters hovered, soft-footed as acolytes. Alice watched the fashionable ladies with secret eyes checking out the little sequined handbags, the swirling chiffon cloaks in jewel colors, the bouffant gowns and those with slim pencil lines. Her clientele back home would benefit from her observations aboard the *Normandie.*

Throughout dinner the two couples spoke casually of the size of the cabins and their en-suite bathrooms, the farewell afforded the ship as it left New York and the triumph of the Joe Louis fight. They avoided the one subject that was probably uppermost in the minds of all the passengers – the possibility of war in Europe.

By the time dessert was served the two couples had moved on to more personal matters.

"Emile, how can you leave your work for six or seven weeks?" Jules asked. "The hair of fashionable ladies will still keep growing."

"Alice needs the rest," said Emile. "Besides, I've left hair styling altogether, *mon oncle,*"

Jules looked surprised. "But you and your partner, what's his name – ah, *oui,* Jacques Laffont, you were doing so well. What of him?"

"Jacques has gone to Hollywood and his ambition is to be the hair stylist to the stars. I'm sure he'll do very well."

"But you'll follow him and make a name for yourself in Hollywood, won't you?"

"I've closed that door forever, I'm afraid. I did something rather rash before I left San Francisco." Emile broke off a piece of baguette and popped it into his mouth. "Anyway, I'm a 'grease monkey' at heart and always will be."

"Really, Emile," said Louise. "A 'grease monkey' indeed. What terrible slang you speak. Anyway, what did you do that was so bad you can't go back to hair styling?"

"Well, you see, *ma tante*, it was like this."

Over coffee Emile told Louise and Jules the story of his last day as a hair stylist. He and Jacques had made a name for themselves at the big departmental store called the White House, situated on the corner of Post and Kearney Streets in San Francisco. It was here he staged his last and unforgiveable act. He told them of a rather troublesome lady who had come in for a cut and perm.

"She insisted on a coiffure quite unsuited to her face," Emile said.

After years of kowtowing to every sort of customer, the lazy, the crazy and everyone in between, Emile Pothron had had enough. He decided to teach this particular client a lesson. He turned her away from the mirror then cut her hair very, very short, so short that in places she was bald. With that grand gesture, and amid hysterical screams from the customer, Emile walked out of the salon and out of his profession as a hairstylist.

It was time for something new, he said.

Emile had no doubt he could make a good living in America. He and Jacques had found it to be just as everyone in Paris had predicted – a land of golden opportunities, provided one was prepared to work hard and grab the breaks as they came.

Jacques Laffont and Emile Pothron had met in 1923 when they were both illegal migrants fighting for a toehold in the new country. Neither could speak English and neither was certain where their next meal would come from. Both had worked on trans-Atlantic freighters and had jumped ship in New York. But they were trained mechanics and quickly found work in the trade. Jacques speculated that having a 'second string to their bow' would be a good idea, so they entered hair styling school and soon qualified.

They both landed jobs working in the evenings at one of the most prestigious salons in New York passing themselves off as hair stylists who had just arrived from Paris.

Their French accents helped in giving them an aura of elegant mystery. It beggars belief that, in spite of their training as hairdressers, two motor mechanics from France could have won the hearts and minds – and heads – of the upper echelons of New York society. It also says much for the charm and affability – and expertise – of the two young Frenchmen that they became so successful.

They did well until 1929 when the Great Depression hit America. A sudden loss of confidence in the economy created havoc and misery. Both Emile and Jacques lost their jobs in the automobile industry but continued their New York hair styling careers, albeit with diminished earnings. They counted themselves lucky to have had the foresight to train for a second career and were not on the dole like so many other desperate men and women.

By 1934, when the economy had picked up a little, the call of the 'Wild West' drew them to San Francisco where they once again succeeded in becoming hair stylists to the elite. They worked in the Antoine Coiffure Salon, a department of the White House which had opened in 1854 and was an icon of the city. Using Emile's 'trade name' of Louis, a contemporary advertisement from the San Francisco Examiner, proclaims:

Monsieur Louis Pothron,
Master in Hair Styling Will Arrive From Paris
And Will Offer the Latest Styles And
Complimentary Consultation.

As they say, it pays to advertise. It was an imaginative bit of PR as Emile had arrived from New York where he had been a mechanic at Hulett Motor Company.

He must have been popular and talented because in four years Emile had become a comparatively wealthy young man and in June 1938 he was on board a luxury cruise liner in the middle of the Atlantic Ocean with his charming wife at his side.

It was all so exciting. Mid-summer and they would soon be back in their beloved France. Any talk of war was silly, Alice thought, just scaremongering and not worthy of attention because thinking about it would only make it real. If she refused to dwell on it then perhaps it would all go away.

War? *Certainement pas*, certainly not.

On board the *Normandie* they were cocooned from all news, good and bad. Shielded from the tragedy about to descend on Europe and into which they were naively sailing, they dined and danced and enjoyed every luxury.

Nothing was going to happen. Of that they were certain.

France had suffered enough during the war of 1914-1918, the one they called the Great War. It had left the country devastated. Everyone said it could not possibly happen again, therefore it would not. France had the best army in Europe and Alice had read about the impregnable Maginot Line.

Besides, the First World War was known as 'the war to end all wars'. The French called it *la der des ders* – the last of the last – and so it would be. There was no need to worry.

But in Europe a nasty case of megalomania was brewing in the black heart and mind of Adolf Hitler.

Strategies were being planned for the take-over of the entire world, the extermination of nations and the enslavement of people.

History was about to be made.

CHAPTER 2

"More capable of heroism than virtue, of genius more
than good sense, they [the French] are suited more to
conceiving immense plans than to completing great
enterprises".
- Alexis de Tocqueville

An early morning arrival at Le Havre in France,
sea mist still clinging to the coastline. Rocky
promontories and buildings seemed to float in the
early morning haze as Alice and Emile watched small
boats heading out to sea for the morning catch.

Tug boats hummed like wasps around an over-
ripe peach as they shoved and worried the *SS
Normandie* towards the pier. A messenger line was
thrown to waiting stevedores who pulled, shouted
and gesticulated until they had hauled the giant
hawsers in and secured them to bollards, satisfied
only when the cruise liner was tucked neatly against
the quay. The crew then maneuvered a covered
walkway into place and the *Normandie's* passengers
finally walked on to solid ground. Even as they
strolled towards the cabs waiting to take them to the
railway station, cranes began hoisting heavily loaded
pallets filled with cargo. Sweating chandlers bustled
around, clipboards in their hands. The *Normandie*
was being prepared for the return journey.

Alice breathed in the sea-laden air and listened
to the music of her native tongue. She felt as if
something deep inside her was resonating to the

inner music of France. She knew that while she was in France she would long for America. But once back in the States, over-washed by the brash hustle of San Francisco and the stark Californian sun, she would be nostalgic for the soft lavender-tinged French countryside. She was not yet ready to admit to the paradox of having one foot in each country and not being able to let go of either.

But this was not the time for deep philosophical enquiry. Alice Pothron was on vacation.

At a nearby railroad station, a train waited to take them to Paris. They took their seats in a first-class carriage for the three-hour trip, Louise and Jules opposite and Skippy safely tucked into the guard's van along with their trunks. Louise and Jules would travel as far as Paris with them but would go on to Sens in the south-east where they had friends and where they planned to spend part of their vacation.

"You must come to Sens, my dear," Louise said. Addresses were hastily exchanged but Alice doubted they would.

If Emile had anything to do with it, they would spend their time as far from Louise and Jules and Sens as possible. He still felt a great deal of resentment towards the woman who had treated them so shabbily. He had first encountered Louise Fromont when she found out he and Alice were courting and had threatened to report him to the immigration authorities. That would have meant deportation and the end of his American dream. Oh yes, Louise Fromont was someone he would prefer to keep at arm's length.

"I want to show you my Paris," Emile whispered holding Alice's hand as the train gathered speed.

"Where I slept under bridges and the streets where I begged for food."

Alice was not sure she wanted Emile to stir up bad memories of his days as a child beggar on the streets of Paris.

"And can we go shopping? Remember, you promised."

"I'll buy you anything you want, *coquette*," Emile said. "Just tell me what is your heart's desire and it's yours."

Alice turned away, oblivious of the luxury carriage, the clickety-clack of the train's wheels and the black cinders racing past the windows. How could she tell Emile that all she really wanted was a child?

She could not understand why she had not been able to go full-term with any of her pregnancies. She often wondered if it was something to do with the hardship she had endured as a child, particularly the eight years spent in the orphanage where she had been nothing more than a slave – and a hungry one at that. All the doctors and specialists they had consulted had remained cheerful and optimistic – in spite of a slight heart murmur that had been detected.

"Now, Mrs. Pothron, you must stop worrying. It will happen when it happens," the last one had said. "Just allow nature to take its course. Why don't you go away on a nice long vacation? Forget about trying to get pregnant. Just go and enjoy a good rest."

It was what they planned to do; put thoughts of a family behind them and live one day at a time in a gloriously warm summer in the country of their birth.

The France to which they returned was still in a state of mourning. It was only twenty years since the cessation of World War I and a sort of general exhaustion was still evident. France was a broken nation, economically as well as in heart and spirit. The people had learned the worst of all lessons – that war solved nothing – and the lesson had been paid for with the blood of their best young men. In Verdun alone, a thousand men were killed each day for fifty-one months, a thousand dead per square meter of blood-soaked ground. The young men who would have gone on to be the fathers, politicians, teachers and landowners, the bright, energetic and inventive entrepreneurs were all dead. France had given of its best and there was nothing left.

France was not the only nation to have suffered enormous deprivation in that war. Britain had lost every single published poet and more besides. In Germany, a whole generation of young writers, thinkers, artists and philosophers had died, leaving a huge spiritual and moral vacuum into which the malevolence of Adolf Hitler had poured.

It was no wonder that popular opinion decreed there would never be another one like it.

The France of the late 1930s to which Alice and Emile returned was, in many ways, pretty much stuck in the nineteenth century. Thirty-four percent of the population was still into subsistence farming, trundling the rural roads by horse-drawn cart as transport was largely non-mechanized. Cities and government offices were only beginning to be equipped with telephones, the network unreliable and primitive. Radios were new-fangled and vulnerable, running on precious and hard-to-come-by valves. Refrigeration was rare, electrification of outlying areas slow. Rural France lived by medieval rules and candlelight.

In rural regions women still washed the family clothing in the traditional manner, in cold water down at the river or in the municipal wash houses. A weekly wash for a family of four could take up to eight hours of back-breaking work. Rural women made their own clothes and many wore wooden clogs, or sabots, instead of leather boots or sandals. There were no supermarkets and no packaged food and French women cooked on coal or wood-fired stoves, most of their food coming from their own gardens or those of their neighbors. City dwellers had it a little easier. Paris, for example, was a modern city comparable with the best in the Western world.

A slow change had begun in the late 1920s. Fashion, for example, whether the forerunner or the result of historical and social changes, was transformed when rayon became the new wool and whalebone corsets gave way to elastic girdles. It meant freedom of movement for women and led to other changes in their lives. In cities, women who were once the domestic help in nineteenth-century households or the dressmaker who traveled to the homes of their wealthy clients now developed into a new middle-class *petits commerces* with premises which customers would visit. They became hairdressers, manicurists and seamstresses situated in small inner-city stores, working for themselves and in their own right. Often this was as a result of widowhood when women had to dig deep to find their own resources. Nineteenth century traditions and expectations were breaking down and when women changed their status men were reluctantly forced to follow suit. Although French women only gained the vote in 1945, by the mid-30s they were beginning to flex their economic muscles and this was to have surprising results in the war years when women played an important role in the economic welfare of the nation.

The train traveled slowly towards the small town of Argenteuil on the outskirts of Paris where Emile was born and had grown up. After so many years away he longed to see the contours of the village. In later years, Emile tended to look on his life in Argenteuil not as it had been but as he dreamed it should have been. For him, Argenteuil would always be untainted by reality and the passing years.

Emile Pothron was born in 1900, the year of the Paris World Fair where x-ray machines, automobiles called 'horseless carriages' and the new wireless telegraphy were first exhibited to enthusiastic admirers. It was the year when the first stretch of *le Métro*, from Porte Vincennes to Porte Maillot in Paris, was opened. None of this, however, would have made much impression on the poverty-stricken Pothron family.

Emile was the fourteenth of fifteen children. Their mother, Pauline Muller, died at the age of forty-three while giving birth to the last child. Emile had never spoken of it but the loss must have lain heavily on his young shoulders. Too young for logic, he felt an unreasoning guilt as if he alone had been responsible for her death. His father had said his had been a hard and prolonged birth process leaving his mother exhausted, vulnerable and sickly. The old man swore in bitterness and anger that she had been considerably weakened by Emile's birth, as if it was the child's fault. Emile grew up believing he was the one who had taken away the sole source of love and comfort in their wretched lives.

His sisters cared for him in a state of benign neglect, allowing him to grow wild and scrawny like a weed in the shade. In the way of older brothers he was bullied, had his head rapped by careless knuckles and was teased unmercifully until he became resilient and self-sufficient. He wore everyone's hand-me-down clothes and the only consolation was that all the other boys in the village were likewise dressed. Life was a harsh struggle but they did not complain. Poverty was a given and the only way out was up.

Alice did not have the heart to say that was how it had been for all children. A big family was part of the economic necessity of the time, especially in rural areas where children were expected to work in order to feed the family. Then when they grew up they looked after their parents. It had always been so. It was only when education became universal that children had prospects beyond the fields. Modern health care also reduced child mortality and, later, birth control gave women the opportunity to be more than just baby-making machines as his mother had been.

Unlike Alice's family, Emile's people had not always been poor. In the early days the Pothron clan owned vast and profitable vineyards around Argenteuil. They also produced large white asparagus; a special delicacy in Parisian restaurants. Unfortunately, in 1888, Phylloxera decimated grape vines throughout Europe. Argenteuil was particularly hard hit and the Pothron family lost everything, finally being obliged to work on their own land as laborers.

When they turned twelve the boys joined their father in the fields but, even with his sons working beside him, *Monsieur* Pothron could barely earn enough to feed his large family. It was a hardscrabble kind of life.

The time was fast approaching when Emile would have to leave school and join his brothers in the vineyards. For him there were two choices; either to live in servitude to the grapes or run away and hope for a better life somewhere else. At the age of twelve he left for Paris where he existed for two miserable years as a beggar on the streets.

There were always a lot of them, he told Alice. All dirty little beggars roaming the streets looking for a crust in the garbage cans behind the swell restaurants, a spare franc lying in the gutter or a job and a meal. Some resorted to petty crime. A few francs from someone's pocket could mean the difference between living and dying of hunger.

Alice knew very little of Paris. When she left France in 1924 with her aunt there had been no time to act the tourist. *Tante* Louise wanted to get back to New York as quickly as possible with her twenty-year-old niece in tow. They came in to Paris from Besançon on one steam train, changed to another at a large railway station and made their way to Le Havre and the *SS De Grasse* that transported them to New York. It had all happened too swiftly to gather names or memories. Alice's experience of Paris had been a fleeting one.

Her life in New York in the home of Louise and Jules had been just another chapter of servitude. She was prepared to be a dutiful and loving daughter, even at twenty, when Louise finally acknowledged her existence and came to France to rescue her from the misery of orphanage life. But disillusionment soon set in when she found that all Louise wanted was a live-in maid. The only time she was allowed out of the apartment was when she ran errands. Because she could not speak English very well she was at the mercy of her aunt and uncle.

18

Sitting in the train on the way to Paris with Emile holding her hand, she still felt a frisson of anger at being so ill-treated. But it was over and she was here, in France, and she was with Emile. Nothing else mattered.

Unusual summer heat scorched Paris that year. There was so much to see – monuments, churches and museums – that even record temperatures could not quell their enthusiasm. Alice pranced along the streets of Paris like a young colt, pulling Emile along in her eagerness to see and do everything.

Paris was in a celebratory mood. France was about to play host to King George VI and Queen Elizabeth of England. The visit had been scheduled for June but Her Majesty's mother, the Countess of Strathmore, had died suddenly and so the visit was re-scheduled for 19 – 22 July. Even then there were doubts the visit would take place as the King had also been ill.

Everyone breathed a sigh of relief when the visit went ahead in spite of the setback to His Majesty's fragile health.

The city had prepared itself well for the official engagement which, everyone knew, was to strengthen *entente cordiale* between France and Britain in the face of Germany's increasing hostility. Hands across the English Channel or, as the French called it, *la Manche.*

Paris was ablaze with Union Jacks and the Tricolor hanging side-by-side from every lamppost. Red and white geraniums dazzled from window boxes and the streets, trams and stores bustled with excited citizens. Stores had decorated their windows with symbols of fraternity between the two nations and the joy at receiving the popular and handsome

Royal couple. As it was a particularly hot summer, everyone wondered if Queen Elizabeth would wear customary black mourning. Parisians gasped when Her Majesty stepped from the motor launch at the Hotel de Ville dressed in brilliant white. Alice noted with interest the sweep of her dress and, later, was entranced by photographs of the Queen's white crinoline ball gown.

The gaiety was contagious. Alice and Emile were pulled into the celebrations, joining in the all-night dancing along the decorated streets and carousing with Parisians whose names they did not know and whose faces were unfamiliar, but smiling. At the Scheherazade nightclub they viewed the semi-naked dancers in the popular floor show, walked back to their hotel as the sun came up and fell into bed exhausted and happy.

Each day they tramped the length and breadth of Paris, taking in the sights, sounds and smells. They plunged down the steps to the Metro, jumped on trams, watched sidewalk artists painting on the bank of the river Seine. On Sunday they took the Metro to the *jardins des Tuileries* where a brass band played the *chansons* of Charles Trenet, Edith Piaf and Maurice Chevalier.

Arm-in-arm they wandered down tree-lined *boulevards*, bought fresh *croissants* from a *boulangerie* and boldly ate them as they strolled along the cobblestone streets. At sidewalk cafés they drank coffee in small cups and felt *oo-la-la* so cosmopolitan.

As they passed the large *Les Grands Magasins du Printemps* department store Alice pulled on Emile's arm until he reluctantly followed her inside. The expression on his face said it all. He would write the check and carry the parcels, nothing more. An hour later they ambled out into the summer sun, arms parcel-laden and with Emile wearing a jaunty new straw boater in the style of the singer Maurice Chevalier.

"Now you look like a real Frenchman," Alice said.

"I am a real Frenchman," Emile replied.

Alice reluctantly allowed Emile to take her to the less salubrious areas of Paris. Here the buildings were dingy, the streets and gutters littered with garbage. No bright festivities here, only ground-down poverty.

When Emile returned to Argenteuil after having lived on the streets of Paris for two years, the Great War had begun. In those two years there had been great changes in his home; everyone had gone. His sisters had married and moved away and his father and brothers were in the army where they would all eventually die in the bloody trenches of the Somme, Passchendaele and Verdun. The only sister left in Argenteuil was Madeleine, so she and her husband, consumptive and ailing, gave Emile a home. But he had to pay his way and so, at the age of fourteen, Emile went to work at the Lorraine Dietrich automobile factory.

The village of Argenteuil had its moment of glory when, in 1871, the artist Claude Monet lived in a small house by the river. Over an eight-year period he painted almost one hundred of his best loved paintings, all from his floating studio on the Seine at Argenteuil. He was visited by most of the great artists of his generation, including the impressionists Èdouard Manet, Alfred Sisley and Vincent van Gogh. While visiting his friend Monet, Pierre-Auguste Renoir painted the now-famous 'The Oarsmen's

Breakfast' depicting a popular Argenteuil haunt that Emile and his family had often visited and which Emile now studiously avoided – fearful of sad memories.

He found the work at the Lorraine Dietrich automobile factory much to his liking. He discovered a natural aptitude that would serve him well in the future. In order to further his technical education he left Lorraine Dietrich a year later and went to work for the Clement Bayard Company at Levallois-Perret, Paris. At the time the company manufactured high-quality motor vehicles as well as military airships. In 1917 he left Clement Bayard for Hispano-Suiza in the suburb of Bois-Colombes in Paris, a company whose luxury automobiles were popular with the European elite. When Emile worked there aircraft engines were also rolling off the assembly line and there is no doubt that, given his post-war career at the Naval Air Base in Alameda, California, he also trained in aircraft technology.

At the time the Great War raged on in northern France and aircraft were just beginning to make their mark. Initially used as ancillary to the cavalry and the artillery for reconnaissance, they would later be utilized for air-to-ground attack. Airplanes were about to change the face of modern warfare and Emile Pothron was at the heart of it.

Working with engines and tools, covered in grease and smelling of motor oil, Emile had found his niche and was a happy young man. Not only was he earning a wage and paying rent to his sister, but he was doing a job for which he was eminently suited. He became a skilled motor mechanic and auto-electrician and these skills would serve him well in the next step of his dream.

Emile Pothron wanted to go to America. He wanted it so badly he could taste it; smell the mustardy scent of chaparral and see wide-open spaces where he imagined wild ponies danced, feel the Californian sun beating on his shoulders. He dreamed of the opportunities that would open up for him. America was a land with gold underfoot, a country where anything was possible. That was what he had heard in Paris from vacationing sailors and he was happy to believe every word of it. At first he thought he would stow away on a ship. But now that he had good qualifications it would be easier to go legitimately as a seaman onboard a freighter. When he got to the Statue of Liberty (yes, he had heard about that too) he would jump ship and nothing would stop him from becoming an American millionaire – just like they said in Paris.

But in 1919, much to his disappointment, he was drafted into the French Army. The law stated every young man had to serve and so he reluctantly left Hispano-Suiza and made his way to the army barracks at Versailles in Paris. There he worked as a radiologist until 1921 when he was twenty years old. Once again, this experience was to impact on his future.

Although the Great War had ended the year before his conscription, there were still men in hospital suffering horrendous and slow-healing wounds of body and mind. There was no penicillin, surgery was fairly primitive and men could – and did – die of septicemia or other infections. For many the war would never be over. Emile and those in his medical unit saw broken spirits as well as broken bodies; especially among those who had fought at Verdun. For this was the place spoken of in hushed tones as the worst that man could endure.

Emile in 1919

About four million men, more than half those who had survived, had suffered terrible injuries or were incapacitated in some way. They were the venerated and ubiquitous symbols of France's travail. No wonder people found themselves infected by what they called a 'long siege of black sorrow'. Each day they faced the results of war, in their homes and on their streets. The whole nation suffered a form of post-traumatic stress and it was to have dreadful consequences when once again they were faced with a German invasion.

When Alice and Emile were in Paris in July and August 1938 they heard whispers of a new and terrible war gathering pace across Europe and saw the face of fear lurking beneath Parisian gaiety. Many suspected they were being kept in the dark by their leaders about the real state of affairs, or that their leaders did not know or acknowledge the reality of the situation. It had a detrimental effect on people as it led, on one hand, to dramatic and exaggerated rumor, or worse, to blind optimism.

There was a nagging fear that war would not be contained by a designated battlefield as in the past but would spew out into the civilian population. People knew the horrors of that sort of warfare from what had happened in the Spanish Civil war where there had been aerial bombing of civilians at places like Guernica. This previously unknown type of warfare meant civilians were vulnerable to attack in their homes, not only from ground troops but from the air. In a new war, innocent civilians and cities would become prime targets and none was more important or more vulnerable than Paris with its sprawling administration and invaluable treasures.

Optimistically people spoke of the Maginot Line, the huge defensive fortification that stretched from Switzerland to Luxembourg along the French/German border. They praised it as if it were the magic line that had been drawn in the sand. No German could cross into France, they declared, because the Maginot Line was impregnable. After all, it had cost three billion francs to build therefore it had to be good. People also spoke of the three million French soldiers already called to arms. But above all they tried to ignore the doomsayers.

There would never be another war with Germany, they cried. It cannot be. *Non, non.*

But there was an ominous rumbling and an unsettling cloud on the horizon.

CHAPTER 3

"Men should have a fear of the loneliness of orphans and of the souls of their departed parents. A man should love the unfortunate orphan of whom he is guardian as if he were his own child."

- Plato

The world had been warily watching Hitler's power-play from the time he became Chancellor of Germany in 1933. Almost immediately his dreaded 'brown shirts' had begun to plague the streets like rats gnawing at the fabric of ordered life. They were bullies and enforcers who targeted the weak and vulnerable, but especially the Jews.

In 1936, Hitler had moved his army into the Rhineland, far too close to France for comfort. In 1937, he withdrew from the Treaty of Versailles which had, theoretically, restricted Germany from forming an effective army, air force and navy. Despite the Treaty, Germany had re-armed and possessed the finest, most disciplined and best equipped army in Europe. In 1938, Hitler annexed Austria and then in 1939, Germany marched into Czechoslovakia.

Another war was inevitable.

It gave Alice and Emile a false sense of assurance that Parisians were so adamantly denying the possibility of another war. In an atmosphere of false confidence, they went about enjoying their holiday. They had promised themselves that part of their vacation would be spent trying to find lost members of their families and so the first visit they made was to Argenteuil, now a suburb of a rapidly expanding Paris. There they found Madeleine had died and was buried in the cemetery that had, ironically, once been part of the Pothron land. Emile's brothers were all dead and he did not know where his other sisters were so he sadly agreed with Alice that he had reached the end of his search. But there was one more family member to find. Henri Guyonvernier, Alice's brother.

They decided to buy an automobile; a black Citroën which, they cheerfully and unashamedly agreed, was a status symbol of the first order. It was an extravagance given the uneasy future of Europe and the fact they were only staying in France for six weeks. But they shrugged and went on enjoying themselves in benign ignorance of the future. When they had their fill of Paris they motored through the autumn fields, past small grey villages, finally reaching Paron, near Sens, where *tante* Louise and *oncle* Jules had bought a house.

They had been summoned to attend a family conference. Louise had received the news that a sister had died and they needed to talk about the children. The eldest boy was eighteen and he had offered to take on his seventeen year-old brother. One girl wanted to join the convent.

"I shall take Paulette," said Louise. "She can help me around the house."

Alice felt cold, as if an ill-forgotten ghost had brushed passed her leaving a snail's-trail of sadness on her shoulders. It had the nasty feel of *déjà-vu* and it looked as if Paulette was about to suffer the same fate as Alice had in the 'care' of Louise Fromont.

That left Jean. He was one year-old and Louise was at a loss as to what to do with the toddler. His teenage brother could hardly be expected to make a home for a baby. The sister, as far as Louise was concerned, was a dead loss, going into the convent. She was avoiding responsibility for her baby brother, Louise said, not without some justification.

"I certainly can't take him," said Louise. "So I suppose he'll just have to go into the orphanage."

Alice was appalled. How could a one year-old child cope with the loss of all he had known and loved? How could he adapt to the severe life of an orphanage, the coldness, the rigidity and overcrowding? She and her brothers, Gaston and Henri, had learned the hard lessons of orphanage life. Henri had told her what they had been through and six year-old Gaston had died as a result. Or so Alice believed.

It looked as if Alice and Emile would never have a child of their own, so why not adopt this unwanted little boy? Was this perhaps the solution? They talked it over and made a decision. It looked as if the child would be taken care of, after all.

One morning soon after that conversation, Louise came to them, a smirk outlining her teeth. Alice knew that look. Louise was up to something.

"I've some news for you," she said at last. "I've found Henri."

For a moment Alice was stunned. "Henri? Henri Guyonvernier, my brother?"

"Yes. He's still in Besançon, not far from the orphanage where you grew up. He's working at some bar or the other. Menial work, no doubt," Louise said, giving a contemptuous little sniff.

She had always thought her sister Maria's three children would come to no good and it appeared that, in Henri, the prediction had come true. She was withholding her verdict on Alice. She had done her best by the girl and then she had gone and married this man who called himself a 'grease monkey' and who played at hair styling. Well, really. She had tried to stop the marriage, even threatened to report Emile to the authorities. But they had outsmarted her, slipping all of Alice's belongings out of the apartment behind her back and getting married on the sly. She was not one to forget.

Alice was in no doubt she would have to pay for this information although Louise's action may have been prompted by their generosity in taking on the unwanted child.

"I have his address," Louise said. "Here, I'll write it down for you."

Alice hugged the piece of paper to her chest, heart too full to articulate her thanks. They would go to Besançon as soon as they could and she would throw her arms around her brother and never let go.

Alice was born on 25 January 1904, the eldest of the three Guyonvernier children. Their father, Joseph, was an impoverished coal miner drafted into the French Army at the beginning of the Great War. He left a sickly wife in the care of their eight year-old daughter, Alice. He died early in the war, his resting place unknown. Her mother, Maria Fromont, died in 1915. It was wartime and there was no one either in the village or in the family prepared to stretch the potatoes, soup and bread to include three newly orphaned children.

At the age of eleven Alice was placed in the Catholic Community Orphanage at Besançon. Her two brothers, Henri aged nine and Gaston aged six, went to the boy's orphanage. The immediate problem of the orphaned Guyonvernier children had been solved, although their future in these supposedly safe refuges was dire.

France had already been at war for two years. Food was short and the whole population suffered hunger and deprivation. Available food naturally went to the fighting men. The orphanages may have been models of rectitude but they quickly became receptacles for the abandoned children of families decimated by disease, poverty and war. No matter how good the intentions, many children died of malnutrition, disease, harsh punishment, overcrowding and possibly plain neglect.

For Alice, the conditions in the orphanage seemed unjustly cruel. She was expected to help with the care of the babies and younger children. She mended their threadbare clothing. She learned to sew simple aprons and smocks cut from the old habits of the nuns or from donations already worn out. The children's clothing had to be washed in the river, and on winter days, Alice and some of the older girls had to break ice from the river's edge before they could get to work.

Ironing was another chore. The big irons were heated on the stove and cleaned of coal dust before they could be used. It was back-breaking labor.

She also worked in the kitchen under the beady eyes of the nuns. While she was spared the cooking roster, she spent most of her time in the kitchen where at least it was warm in winter. In summer the steaming kitchen was the Hell she had heard about in Bible lessons.

She rarely saw her brothers as they were confined in a separate grey stone building under the dubious care of the brothers. On Sundays the children were herded into the local church where they would smile at each other and whisper when they could. Henri was a compliant child, wise enough to know, if he wanted to survive, he had better keep his head down. At six years-old Gaston was rebellious and intent on pushing the boundaries of his world. On Sundays Alice would see new cuts, abrasions and bruises. She worried as Gaston limped into church. She feared he was getting beaten too hard and too often, concerned that something dreadful would happen.

And it did.

At church one Sunday Henri was alone. Alice looked across the crowded pews and Henri shrugged. Gaston was gone and he was never seen again. Alice always believed he had died under the harsh treatment meted out to him by the brothers at the orphanage. She had no proof and when it was said that Gaston had run away she could not verify the truth of the statement. If they had admitted the child had died of measles, scarlet fever, diphtheria, pneumonia or some other prevalent disease, her fears may have been allayed. Instead, to her dying day, she believed her brother had been killed by those charged by God and the State to look after him. It was a sinister death, possibly only created in the mind of a sensitive, over-imaginative, lonely little girl but it was to haunt Alice all her life.

Henri was fourteen years old and had been in the orphanage for five years when he began to talk of running away. He begged Alice to go with him. He explained how he was going to get out. The great doors were always locked and most windows barred. But he had found one window high in a neglected attic no one had noticed. It was unbarred and opened onto a sloping roof he thought he could descend. He would wait for a stormy night when the wind shrieked around corners and trees scraped at the windows. Then he would clamber onto the roof and work his way to a point where he could jump down in comparative safety, especially if snow had drifted up in piles against the wall.

"I can do it, Alice. You must find a way to get out too. We'll go together and we'll be free," he urged. "I can work. I'm strong. We'll be together and we'll be safe."

But Alice shook her head. Too afraid of the unknown, she stayed in the orphanage long after Henri had made his escape. It was a sad time for her as she was convinced she would never see her brother again.

But now she had an address! She was ecstatic and begged Emile to take her to Besançon at the first possible moment.

While Alice and Emile travelled south to Besançon the wheels of history continued to turn. On the 4 September 1938 William Bullitt, the American Ambassador to France, unveiled a plaque at Point-de-Garve celebrating Franco-American friendship. He stated that France and the United States were united in war and peace, giving the impression that, should Hitler invade, America would go to war for France. Emile and Alice were elated but five days later F D Roosevelt, the American President, refuted Bullitt's optimism by saying that America would remain neutral. In France there was a collective sigh of disappointment but Roosevelt was only echoing the will of the American people who wanted nothing to do with any future European conflict. The general consensus in America was; 'been there, done that, never again'.

Privately, Emile could not blame them. Why should they get themselves involved in someone else's war? They had done it once and had lost one hundred and seventeen thousand men in the process; a small percentage of the fifteen million military personnel who had died in the Great War, but each one an American boy who never went home.

On 30 September 1938, a treaty was signed in Munich between France, Britain, Germany and Italy. It was agreed the Sudetenland in north-west Czechoslovakia would be ceded to Germany. Neville Chamberlain, then British Prime Minister, went back to London with the message 'peace in our time'.

It looked like war had been averted.

'Now perhaps Hitler's appetite will be satisfied,' was the general feeling both in France and Britain. But there were grave doubts among the skeptics, including the belligerent Winston Churchill who was First Lord of the Admiralty. In a speech to the House of Commons in London he said to Prime Minister Chamberlain, "You were given the choice between war and dishonor. You chose dishonor, and you will have war."

Unaware of the unfolding of history, Emile and Alice drove to Besançon, an old garrison town close to the Swiss border and nestled in the foothills of the Jura Mountains. They travelled through vineyards and fields, savoring the richness of autumn colors. It was late August and France seemed at its most beautiful. The trees along the roads were on fire with red and gold leaves, cattle in the fields looked on with calm contemplation as they passed.

They crossed over the river Doub in their brand new auto, marveling at the gracious riverside buildings whose reflections pulsed in the soft-flowing waterway. They laughed at the oarsmen who rocked and cursed as the frosty wakes of faster craft threatened to overturn them. They smiled and waved at the men on cargo boats as they chugged loudly under the stone bridges.

When they finally found the small bar in which Henri worked, Alice was in a ferment of doubt. She was not even sure she would recognize her brother after all these years. But when she saw Henri behind the counter of the bar all her worries faded. He looked up from the glass he was drying, stared at her for a long moment and then his dear familiar face creased into a broad grin. He stretched out his arms as if to catch her.

"Mon Dieu," he said. "Alice."

It was a time of unprecedented happiness; back in France, the land of her birth, with her beloved Emile, and now to have found her brother made Alice's life complete. Mr. Chamberlain's news that war had been averted convinced them that the dreaded cloud of conflict no longer hung over them. It gave her such a sense of peace and relaxation that the unimagined happened.

Alice discovered she was pregnant.

Despite their incredulous joy, once again the specter of miscarriage hung over her. The doctor they visited in Sens was adamant.

"You have had three miscarriages and I pick up a slight heart murmur," he said. "Did you know about that?" When Alice nodded he went on. "That means your health is already severely compromised. You must consider nothing less than total bed rest if you wish to carry this child to full-term."

This baby had to have the best opportunity to survive. It would probably be their last chance as Alice was now thirty four years-old and it was almost too late. Her health was fragile, possibly due to childhood malnutrition, three miscarriages and the heart defect. She found it difficult to fight off infection and, as a consequence, suffered frequent bouts of bronchitis that often turned into full-blown pneumonia. The doctor's advice of bed-rest made sense. Although they were due to board the *Normandie* in two weeks Alice and Emile decided to stay in France until after the birth of their child.

Adopting the one-year old Jean now seemed out of the question. Alice was in no position to care for him and so it was with heavy hearts they agreed he should go into an orphanage, at least for the time being. Once over the pregnancy and when Alice was strong again they would reconsider the situation. It felt like Jean's future was one problem too many and they set it aside to be considered later. Emile thought they would have time to make such decisions once the baby was born and Alice had regained her health. But history changed their circumstances and Jean disappeared into the orphanage and was lost to them forever.

As winter arrived and drew circles of snow in the fields Emile found a small farmhouse to rent. It was in Fouchere, just outside Paron and close to where Louise and Jules were now living. The farm was owned by Monsieur Auguste Delajon and his wife Albertine Garby. The name of the farm, *à la belle etoile,* translated into 'out in the open air' or 'under the stars', and augured well for the success of the pregnancy.

For months Alice lay in bed surrounded by the harmony and sweetness of country life; first the crystalline snow that blanketed the garden then, as spring came, the crowing of a rooster curling through the early morning mist, the sound of bees in the apple trees and the perfume of lavender. As she grew stronger and her baby grew within her, warm and safe, it was as if she had absorbed the fecund French countryside into her being and it had made her whole.

Emile re-arranged their return tickets. They would be on the *Normandie* at the end of September 1939 at the very latest – a year later than they had planned. But they would be going home with the greatest gift of all, a newborn baby. Emile was determined to give their child the best chance possible – even if it meant tying Alice to the bed for six months!

Emile acknowledged Alice's frustration at not being able to get out and about. Each Sunday he smilingly granted Alice 'leave-of-absence' from her bed. As spring then summer flushed the countryside with warmth and life, he allowed her to sit outside under an old grapevine that tendriled its way across the veranda. As fall stripped the trees and carpeted the ground with new falls of snow they sat on the sofa in front of a fire. It was there that Emile discussed whatever news he felt Alice ought to hear. Fending off her questions was another matter.

"But what of this smart-aleck Italian?" she demanded. "What is his claim to fame?"

"He calls himself 'His Excellency Benito Mussolini, Head of Government, Duce of Fascism, Founder of the Empire and First Marshal of the Empire'," Emile told her with a grin. He had read Mussolini's preposterous self-aggrandizement in the newspaper and, like many others, underestimated the Fascist dictator's ability to cause mayhem. "He's a bit of an upstart but popular – like Hitler."

"In what way?"

"Well, for one thing he got the Italian railroad to work. I believe the trains now run on time."

Alice laughed. "Emile, really. He must have done more than just fix the train schedules."

"Yes, I suppose he has. But the man's a jackal, hoping for a chew at the cadaver of Europe. He's going to be trouble."

This was prophetic because, on 22 May 1939, Hitler and Mussolini announced a formal alliance.

War had just crept one step closer.

CHAPTER 4

Only mothers can think of the future –
because they give birth to it in their children.
                                        - Maxim Gorky

In the early hours of Thursday 8 June 1939, Alice went into labor. Emile subdued his panic and placed her carefully on the back seat of the Citroën and, in the quiet of a country dawn, he drove her to the hospital at 7 place de L'abbe Gregoire in Sens. She had carried to full term but was she strong enough to come through the final ordeal?

Emile had heard so many stories of women dying in childbirth. His own mother had died giving birth and he had witnessed her suffering in that small crowded house where she had not even been able to go through her travail in private.

He strode the hospital corridors in a frenzy of suspense. Finally, at 1.35 pm Alice gave birth to a daughter, Evelyne Claudette.

To Emile's enormous relief both mother and child had come through reasonably well. A week later, when the doctors were confident that Alice was strong enough, Emile drove his new family back to Fouchere. There, secluded from the world and ignorant of the more urgent mutterings of war, Emile cared for Alice and marveled at the beauty and fragility of their newborn child.

By the end of August, Emile judged that Alice was almost well enough to travel. They were both excited at the prospect of returning to America where both mother and child would receive the best medical care available. Not only was he spurred on by the excitement of taking their child back to America, but there was also the imminent threat of war that he could no longer ignore. There were daily reports in the newspapers and on the radio, some of which had to be true: that Hitler's powerful army was mowing down small nations across Europe in a scythe of frenzy and malice. In March 1939, Germany invaded Czechoslovakia. In April Italy took Albania.

Things did not look good.

Alice assured Emile she felt well enough to travel although she looked far from well as this photograph below attests.

Alice and Evelyne

Another month, she reckoned, and she would be absolutely fine. Emile was not sure they had a month so he decided to go to Paris and confirm their return passage on the *Normandie.* They would leave on the first available crossing.

But it was already too late.

On 1 September 1939, Germany invaded Poland. Because Britain, her Dominions and her Allies (including France) had signed a mutual assistance pact with Poland, they were obliged to declare war on Germany. It was a dreadful moment in world history, one that was never supposed to happen after the carnage of World War I.

Once again the world was being dragged into the open mouth of that bloody predator called war.

No country, other than Germany, was ready for a full-scale conflict. America stuck to its isolationist policy (though this was not the personal philosophy of Franklin D Roosevelt who had foreseen the coming catastrophe). Britain's Prime Minister, Neville Chamberlain, still clung to the hope that the Munich Agreement would somehow stick and Hitler would pull back at the last moment, mindful of his obligations to world peace.

But it was not to be. Hitler had promised his people they would be the *übermenschen*, the supermen of the planet. They would carve a place in history that he believed they deserved. Europe and then the world would be conquered so that they, the superior Aryan race, could have it all. They would treat the people they conquered as slaves and exterminate those who were unnecessary. With this mindset, war and genocide was inevitable.

On 2 September 1939, posters appeared in every shop window in France, in the railway stations and on the Paris Metro. It was an announcement of general mobilization. The French army, navy and air force were called to arms.

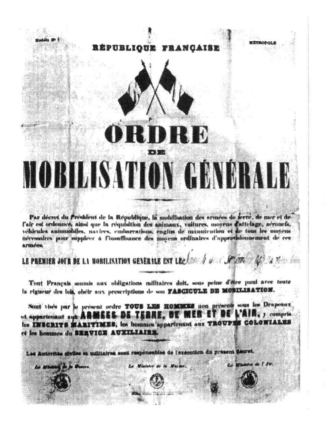

Mobilization poster

Emile Pothron was a worried man. Would they be able to get out of France now that war had been declared? And what was his status as a naturalized American? Alice tried to reassure him. He was no longer a Frenchman, whatever his heart told him. He was an American and had the passport to prove it. He had lived in America for sixteen years. Surely that would count for something and he would avoid the draft? Emile decided to call on the American Ambassador in Paris for clarification of his situation.

On 3 September 1939, Emile took a train to Paris and went to the American Embassy near place de la Concorde. He found the city in an uproar. People were scurrying everywhere like ants from an overturned anthill. Women pushed prams loaded with groceries and howling babies. Anxious families ran towards the railways stations with bulging suitcases. Cabs pulled away from curbs and just as soon were back, filling up again with apprehensive passengers.

Emile was fortunate. The Ambassador, Mr. William Bullitt, was available and Emile set out his problem. He hoped Bullitt would reassure him that he and his family could get on a passenger ship and return to America without further delay.

But Bullitt had bad news for Emile. There were no ships leaving France for New York. And worse, as Emile had been born in France, he was eligible for the draft and would shortly be conscripted into the French Army. There was nothing he could, or would, do for the anxious man standing in front of him.

"You're a day late. The general call-up was issued yesterday, M. Pothron. The *Normandie* sailed from Le Havre on 16 August and will probably be held in New York until things sort themselves out."

"No *Normandie*? Then another ship, perhaps..."

Bullitt shook his head and Emile left the Embassy a deeply troubled man.

If Bullitt was correct there was no way he could get Alice and the baby out of France before the impending conflagration.

Unfortunately, Bullitt never suggested to Emile that perhaps he should try to get his family onto a ferry crossing the Channel to England, where they would have been comparatively safe for the duration of the war. Emile would not have been aware that the ferries were still running but Bullitt should have known. Or perhaps he did. William Bullitt was allegedly anti-British, a disastrous trait he shared with America's Ambassador to Britain, Joseph Kennedy, who hated the British, but worse still, was pro-Nazi. Neither man believed that Britain would stand up to Adolf Hitler. Britain was without weapons and had no hope of withstanding a German invasion. Both men smugly predicted England would soon be under the jackboot of the Nazis where they belonged.

Before things came to a climax a year later in June 1940, the US Secretary of State, Cordell Hull, would send several pressing telegrams to William Bullitt urging him to follow the French government into exile, where he might have been instrumental in changing the defeatist mindset of the nervous and distracted ministers of state. There was a small window of opportunity where Bullitt could perhaps have changed the course of history. Instead, perhaps enthralled by his self-appointed role as "host" to the German invaders and also by his personal friendship with Roosevelt, Bullitt would infamously telegraph Hull: "*J'y suis. J'y reste*" – here I am, here I remain.

Without knowing the future or being aware of the inner machinations of his government and their attempts to get Bullitt to behave, Emile had taken the measure of the man and had found him wanting. More importantly, William Bullitt's general lack of helpfulness would lead directly to great misfortune for the Pothron family.

Emile left Paris on the first available train from Paris to Sens. It was loaded with men making their way to their mobilization points. Women and crying children also crowded into the carriages, hurrying out of Paris to friends or relatives in the country, as if war was already upon them. From the train window Emile noticed the roads were clogged with private vehicles racing away from the city, as well as army personnel carriers transporting troops to the border areas.

In Sens shoppers scurried about, dashing from one store to the other, arms filled with parcels; bumping into one another, their eyes filled with misgiving. The town was like an over-kicked bee hive, all panic and no plan.

Emile returned to Fouchere with a heavy heart. He knew he was bringing Alice some very bad news. He was not sure how she would take the information that, because he was born in France, he would possibly, no, certainly, be drafted. They had missed escaping by such a small margin – only days. Emile's thoughts were for Alice and the new baby. Where would they live? Where would they be safe? How could he care for them if he was drafted? He was concerned about Alice's already fragile health and the shock she would surely sustain at his news.

But Alice already knew they were not going to get out of France before war overtook them. She said nothing as he walked into the kitchen, just pointed to the brown envelope lying like an evil portent on the table. He slit it open with his fingers and read the dreaded news. He had been ordered to report for duty, to the Versailles medical section. He was to return immediately to Paris.

Their lives were about to change forever.

An element of disbelief hung over their reluctant preparations. They discussed ways in which they could escape, tearing at the problem, dragging it this way and that. Spain? No, that country was still trying to get back on its feet after the Civil War. It would not be safe. And in any case, Spain was beholden to Germany that had aided Generalissimo Franco in his triumph. Portugal was an unknown quantity, as was North Africa. What about Algiers, Alice asked. Emile shook his head. Stay here with me, Alice urged. Again Emile shook his head.

The farmhouse at Fouchere
Emile with Evelyne, Alice & Skippy in background

He knew he could not ignore the call-up papers. To do so would be an act of desertion and he would probably be treated to a blindfold and a pitted wall.

Another deciding factor was William Bullitt, who professed knowledge of these things. He certainly did not think trying to get out was a good idea and had urged Emile to do his civic duty.

"So, we're stuck," Alice said her voice flat with finality.

Only twenty years previously the Great War had decimated their families and destroyed their childhood. Neither Alice nor Emile had received the education they deserved or the security that comes from a stable environment. Now history was repeating itself and they could not help but wonder whether their daughter would face the same problems and challenges they had. At that moment life seemed very unfair.

Emile left Alice in the farmhouse at Fouchere and returned to Paris. He was officially inducted into a medical unit, but was given compassionate leave to go home and sort out his affairs. War had been declared but war was not being waged so there was time for the men to make arrangements for their loved ones. Emile hastily returned to the farmhouse and Alice.

It was then he decided to buy a house in Paron where Louise Fromont and Jules Duxin had settled. In this way Alice would at least have family close by, however much she disliked her aunt and uncle.

Earlier Louise had mentioned a house in Paron, just along the road from where they lived and suggested they have a look at it. She pointed it out to them, explaining that none of the houses had an address such as Alice and Emile were used to. In America houses had numbers and streets had names. In French villages, streets had no names and houses no numbers. Instead, each house had a title. Louise's house was *Villa des Oiseau* or Villa of the Birds. The house that Emile would finally buy was called *Le Clos de Paron* or the Garden of Paron.

Alice and Emile strolled past it. *A vendre,* a small notice board declared. 'For sale'. It was large, double-storied and sturdy. Its front windows faced the main road to Sens, giving it a feeling of openness. At the bottom of the garden a small outdoor toilet leaned into itself and nearby was a make-shift shed with a swinging door and a warped wooden floor. Ideal for a wine cellar, Emile thought. In the garden a dry well was covered by a large slab of concrete and a new pump had been installed close to the house.

The house in Paron (circa 1946)

There were four bedrooms upstairs, a large kitchen and rooms downstairs that could be used for general living and at least an acre of land that they could turn into a vegetable garden. A dozen hens pecked busily in the shade of a few straggly fruit trees. A small pig, snout twitching, lounged insolently in the shade. There was also a garage for the Citroën, something that immediately caught Emile's attention. Louise said the house had once been used as accommodation for the Chateau's servants and the large garden had fed the Chateau family and staff. It was far from perfect but the best available in the short time Emile had before reporting for duty.

There were several disadvantages. Firstly, there were no stores in Paron – the closest shopping was in Sens, two miles away. Alice would have to walk there as he had not yet taught her how to drive the Citroën.

Secondly, there was no electricity, no bathroom and, most problematical, no water into the kitchen. Alice would have to draw water from the pump in the back yard and carry it into the house. They had been used to all 'mod cons' in America and Emile wondered how Alice would cope with this rural way of life.

An advantage was the small farm opposite. Emile could see people busy collecting eggs, forking hay, a man leading a large black horse into a row of stables behind the house where, Emile later learned, horses and carriages had once been kept for the Chateau. There were pigs and hens and dogs and a lazy cat lying on a sun-warmed wall. This must be the Jochmans family. Louise had mentioned them.

A small steep-roofed chapel across the road would bring comfort to Alice and, tucked behind the church, was a stone-built wash-house where she could take her laundry.

It was not the sort of home Emile had ever imagined they would own but for the moment it was ideal and Emile felt certain that Alice would be safe, close to Louise and Jules, close to the church, close to a farm and within walking distance of Sens. Their Citroën could be stored in the garage until his return. He felt reassured that Alice and the baby would be comfortable and safe until this whole sorry mess had been sorted out, the war won and the men sent home.

One worry, and it was a small one, was the villagers. Emile had begun to realize that there were two narratives of France, two threads on the same spindle. Industrialization had been gradual and the result was a patchy dual economy with a highly concentrated and modern industry in and close to the cities and an almost medieval farming peasantry in the rural areas.

He and Alice were used to cities; bright, mechanized, full of light and action. They had an urban sophistication, a gloss given by ten years of living in America's most glamorous cities; New York, Boston and San Francisco. Although Emile had grown up in a French village, he admitted to knowing only a little about rural people, their daily challenges and their slower, more thoughtful mindset. Life would be at the pace of their wagons, he reasoned. Their lives would revolve around the church, the weekly market and the village hall and he assumed they would be less tolerant of strangers. Emile wondered how they would react to a newcomer like Alice at a time when horizons were closing and tension ever-present. Would she be accepted into this small tight-knit community, wise in the ways of nature but whose horizons were measured by the distance their carts could carry them? Only time would tell.

On the bright side, Alice would at least be among people fiercely opposed to war. While it was not fighting talk, at least they would resist the Germans in whatever way they could. What action that would take, again, only time would tell.

In the week before his return to duty Emile bought the house in Paron, together with some of the furniture, and settled Alice and Evelyne in; chopped wood and stored it for the coming winter and generally did what he could to make Alice's life a little easier in the coming months. Emile also strengthened the walls of the outside lavatory and placed a small hasp and staple lock on the idly swinging door. There was nothing he could do about the water supply. The water pump stood close to the house surrounded by flagstones, clean washed and pitted by the steady leak of water. Alice would just have to fill a bucket every morning and carry it into the house.

One task he undertook with the zeal of ignorance was to kill the pig. It was generally decided in the village that nothing should be left for the Germans to pilfer, not even a small pig. Armed with an axe Emile went out to do battle while Alice waited inside the kitchen, peering nervously through the window. Emile wished the axe was sharper but just how difficult could it be to chop off a pig's head? Emile crept up to the pig as it lay snoring under the tree. Swung. The axe connected. The pig must have sensed danger for it shot to its feet squealing frantically, blood gushing from a superficial wound in its neck. Emile ran after it swinging the axe above his head. In the kitchen Alice collapsed onto a chair, hysterical laughter bubbling through her lips.

"Stop laughing and go for help. Go fetch Monsieur Jochmans," Emile shouted through the kitchen door. "I can't do it on my own!"

M. Jochmans hurried over. "A city boy trying to kill a pig," he muttered, smiling as he took the axe from Emile. "Leave it to me, M. Pothron."

With one swift blow the pig was dispatched and its carcass carried to the Jochmans' property where the farmer did whatever was necessary to cut the pig cadaver into manageable pieces for salting and storing. Alice did not want to know the finer details of pig slaughtering or dissection. For her, pork was something you bought at the store, not killed on your property.

Emile felt more capable of cleaning out the attic where he came across several First World War rifles. He shot the bolt of one and held it up to the light, remembering his two years in the French Army and his youthful pride in being photographed holding a rifle just like this. He was twenty at the time, in uniform and proudly holding a weapon of war. Now that he was a husband and father, the heft of the rifle felt somewhat distasteful.

He brought them down to the kitchen where he and Alice examined them; a rusty Lebel and a Berthier, more modern than the Lebel but, he told her, only loaded three rounds whereas the Lebel loaded eight.

"And this one's different again," Alice said, pointing to a smaller rifle.

"That's a carbine. Easier to use because it's got a shorter barrel. I suspect someone was keeping these as collector's items. Still, they need to go back to the Army."

Alice was incredulous.

"I can't leave them here," Emile said. "Alright, I'll take the bolts out and throw them down the well. They'll never be found there."

"Why not just leave them in the attic?"

"Suppose the Germans come and find them? What then?"

They looked at each other, filled with trepidation, the unspoken words finally out and festering.

CHAPTER 5

"... their [the French] underlying lack of realism, their belief that, if war was unthinkable, then somehow it wasn't going to happen.
The common result was a lack of preparedness reaching beyond the actions of soldiers and politicians into the national psyche itself."

- Ian Ousby

Emile was ready to leave. He had packed a small haversack with his personal belongings; razor, towel, soap, hairbrush and underwear. In it he also placed the photograph of Alice in her dressing gown, obviously still weak but with a tentative smile on her lips, proudly holding Evelyne up to the camera.

He stood in front of the dressing table combing his hair and settling his forage cap at just the right angle. He took it off and combed his hair again, putting off the moment when he had to say the final farewell. Alice gathered up the last of his belongings and pushed them into his pocket. Her lips trembled and her eyes shone with unshed tears. Emile gripped her hands.

"Don't worry, *coquette*. Nothing is going to happen. It's a joke. They have their Siegfried Line and we have our Maginot Line. We are just facing each other and doing nothing. We'll be fine."

"But they've declared war," she cried. "That isn't 'nothing'."

"You'll be safe here. Now, don't forget what I told you, if things go really belly-up, which they won't, go to Nice and we'll meet there."

"But why Nice? Why not stay right here?"

Emile hesitated. If there was an invasion, which he seriously doubted, would Nice be any safer than Paron? He did not know what to do for the best; what advice to give to Alice. He was confused, in a state of conflict. He wanted to stay with Alice and the baby but the emotional ties to the country of his birth were also strong. Such conflicting emotions were beyond his ability to express, even to his wife.

"*Mon Dieu!*" Emile shouted as he swung the haversack over his shoulder. "I've just remembered. The passports. We're supposed to surrender them. Give them to me and I'll take them to the Embassy when I get a chance."

"Oh, no you won't," she said.

Emile's suggestion was met with a ferocious stare. He sighed. He knew that expression and realized it was no good arguing with her once she had made up her mind. Were the passports really necessary? They each had a *carte d'identité.* They had needed them when they bought the house. At the time they filled in all the correct forms, had taken them to the Prefecture with their birth certificates (Emile obtained his from Argenteuil and Alice's from Beure where she had been born). They had the official *Commissaire de Police* stamps with the *Commissaire's* signature. They were legally French with all the responsibilities that entailed which, in Emile's case, meant a call to arms. Surely the *carte d'identité* would be enough?

"Emile, we worked too hard, waited too long to get those passports. And now you want to hand them in? Never."

"You're right," Emile said, after some thought. "They might come in useful. Sometime in the future it could be safer to be an American rather than French."

"We don't know what the future holds," said Alice. "Let's hide them – in case."

Together they walked through the house looking for a suitable place, into the garden, full of wild weeds and vegetables grown rampant. They walked around the water pump and the outdoor lavatory, past the wooden shed that was falling apart, its walls caving into one another like a sigh. Nothing and nowhere felt safe.

It was only when they explored the attic that they finally decided this was the place. The passports, Alice's jewelry and the money, both the American dollars and some French francs, would be hidden in a dusty cobwebbed corner. Emile pushed the documents, wrapped in a piece of old oilcloth, in between the wall and a roof beam. They stood back as Emile dusted off his hands. The precious package would be safe.

Finally on that late September morning, Emile held Alice tightly and she placed her hands on his neck and felt the beat of his pulse under her fingers.

They did not know when they would see each other again. If ever.

His last duty was to pick his beloved Evelyne up. He cradled her in his arms, crooning into her ear, tears pricking his eyelids as he said goodbye.

"*Mon ange, mon petite ange.*" My little angel.

Later, in the train on his way back to Versailles, he wondered why he had made the reckless suggestion of Nice as a place where they could meet.

Emile and Evelyne

If the Germans invaded then even Nice would not be safe. And why would Alice want to leave Paron, where she was near family, and go to a city she had never visited before? How would she get there if fighting broke out? She was unable to drive and the trains would be prime targets for the enemy. Perhaps he should have told her to go to Paris, to the American Embassy where she could at least claim refuge based on her citizenship. However pompous Ambassador Bullit was, surely he would help a stranded mother and child? He might even offer a safe haven.

How could he have been so stupid as to suggest Nice? But it was too late now and the suggestion would hang in the air with unfortunate results.

In the meantime, Emile had a war to fight and he felt reasonably sure that Alice would be safe in Paron until he returned

He went to the barracks situated at the Versailles Palace in what was *la Petite Écurie du roi*, or stables of the King, where he was inspected, his body probed, his hair cut and his soul, it seemed, signed over to the State. He received an ill-fitting uniform and a rather rusty weapon without a bolt or ammunition. He thought of the rifles he had thrown down the well. These were not much better and Emile realized with a chill that France was far from ready to defend itself.

He was inducted into the Fifth Military Medical Section, one of seventy-five men under the command of Captain Delavierre, a medical doctor. Emile had experience with fluoroscopy and x-ray machines during his conscription as a youngster, so Delavierre gave him the task of setting up the same machines and equipment he had last used in 1919 and finding a place to store the delicate x-ray plates.

The prospect of a long and arduous time away from Alice and Evelyne was awful. Emile could not imagine how long it would be before he saw Alice again and it nagged like a bad toothache.

He explained to Dr Delavierre how a simple vacation had turned into a nightmare for him and his wife. If he and Alice had stayed at home in America where they belonged, perhaps they would have followed Jacques to Hollywood and he might even now be styling the hair of the rich and famous. It was a savage thought.

Delavierre laughed and slapped Emile on the back. "You'll be back there soon, *mon fils*. In the meantime we must persevere – for France."

"*Oui*," replied Emile bleakly. "For France."

The *Petite Écurie du roi* of Versailles was at the time of Louis XIV, the stables that held the court's draft and saddle horses and all necessary equipment such as bridles, saddles and reins, carriages and barouches. The monarch owned seven hundred horses stabled in the *Petite Écurie* and at the *Grande Écurie* across the road. At the time of the First World War, the smaller of the stables had been turned into barracks for various medical units and also used as an army hospital. Far from ideal, it was draughty and hygiene was hard to maintain. Twenty years on the situation had hardly improved.

The 'phony war', later called *drôle de guerre* by the French and *sitzkreig* or 'sitting war' by the Germans, created a stand-off that would last for eight months. Unfortunately, it generated a sense of false calm in Western Europe as the two armies tried to outstare each other across their joint border, the Maginot Line and the Siegfried Line to the east.

Four days after France declared war on Germany a half-hearted French military operation had begun in the Rhine River valley area. This was largely to probe the German defenses but also to gain control over the area between the French border and the German lines. German opposition was weak as most of the troops were still engaged in the savaging of Poland. France had gained ground in this petty squabble but on 12 September the Allies halted all offensive action and the French divisions were ordered to retreat.

Emile wrote to Alice, his letters necessarily banal, filled with his daily schedule. He did not (and could not) tell her that he and the other men of the Fifth Military Medical Section at Versailles were kept busy with the wounded brought in from the Saar offensive and fighting in the border region. He felt a certain satisfaction in discovering his previous ability as a radiologist (or, as he described it, 'an x-ray intendant'). He was pleased he had not been put into a fighting regiment for he did not think he could willingly kill another man. It was a disappointment, however, that the medical equipment was not much more advanced than that which he had used in 1919. It seemed as if health practices had stagnated in spite of France's reputation for medical innovation.

The outbreak of the First World War had exposed the deplorable state of public health in France and of recruits in particular. In 1914 consumption – or tuberculosis – accounted for ten percent of all deaths in France. Diphtheria caused high child mortality. In 1918/19 a terrible outbreak of what was called Spanish influenza also took its toll and in France almost half a million men and women died.

Vaccines for various diseases were available but opponents to vaccination, particularly for diphtheria and tetanus, argued that the discoverer of the vaccine, Gaston Ramon at the Pasteur Institute, was a veterinarian by training and could not possibly know anything about medicine for humans.

Innovations and discoveries should have given French medicine the edge, but this was not always the case. In 1816, René Laennec of the *Necker-Enfants Malades* Hospital in Paris invented the precursor of the modern stethoscope. In 1911, Marie

Curie discovered radium. Louis Pasteur founded the science of microbiology when he established a connection between bacteria and disease. He also developed various vaccines. The pasteurization of milk went a long way to preventing TB in humans.

France's contribution to the improvement of health throughout the world was remarkable.

But in France, general practitioners were late in taking these discoveries into their practices. Understandably, local doctors were set in their ways and unwilling to change. It meant that in the early 20th century many men were unfit for the looming war. In 1939, general health had not improved substantially; consequently Emile's unit had more than war wounds to contend with.

The young American soon became popular with the men in his Division. They wanted to know all about America. They had been told America was a land of riches where everyone drove a Cadillac. Was it true? What about the movie stars, Greta Garbo and Jean Harlow? *Très enchanteur!* Did he know them? When he ruefully admitted he did not know either, the others cheerfully slapped his back and said, "*L'américain, il ne sait rien.*" The American, he knows nothing.

Emile did not disclose the fact that, had he not been in uniform in a country on the edge of war, he might very well have got to know both Jean Harlow and Greta Garbo.

Captain Delavierre stood on the side watching the friendly interplay with some amusement. The young American had held his own and did not take exception to the ribbing he got from the others. He liked that in a man.

As time went on Emile developed a special rapport with the older man. Dr Delavierre told him he had seen service at Verdun. He had no illusions about the senselessness of war, having seen the worst. Emile knew next to nothing about his senior, except that he was a pretty good sort.

Little did he know that Captain Delavierre would shortly play a crucial role in his life.

CHAPTER 6

Notices were posted in all brothels ... to the effect
that women [the prostitutes] ... had to take at least
one bath a week ...

- Robert Gildea

The winter of 1939/40 turned out to be one of
the coldest on record with temperatures slithering
down to -19°C (-2°F) in the north and -24° C (-11°F) in
the east where Alice lived. Reportedly the coldest
winter since 1889, bread froze solid and ice gathered
on indoor window sills. Outside, the ground
underfoot clanked like iron.

Food was short. Normal harvesting had been
disrupted. Distribution was inefficient and storing of
grain a problem. Men in the forces also needed to be
fed, which meant less for the general population.
Food shortages were having an adverse effect on
people, leaving them more vulnerable to cold and
illness.

In spite of the lack of food and the seemingly
unending cold, Alice began to enjoy the solitude and
the peace of winter. She took delight in the flower-
patterns of frost on the windows, the crunch of new
snow underfoot when she went to the Jochmans'
farm to collect milk. She loved the smell of wood
smoke that curled through the freshness of the
morning. Cocooned in a brilliant cloak of snow that
muffled sound, even the rich tolling of the church
bells across the river from Sens, she slowly began to

accept Emile's absence and her enforced stay in France.

She learned to chop wood and make up the stove so that they were comparatively warm and snug. She found that a brick, placed in the oven for a while, then wrapped in a thin towel and pushed into the bottom of the bed made an excellent hot water bottle. She taught herself to make bread and looked in wonder at her first loaf, golden and crusty.

With Evelyne asleep in the stroller, she walked the half-empty streets of Paron. She went by the small Café Restaurant du Centre which seemed to be the main hang-out of old men. There they played cards or chess, smoked and drank the local red wine. At the back of the bistro they had set up a *petanque* court where, in summer, fierce games were fought as if the pride and honor of France were at stake. Sometimes the soft voice of an accordion would draw out a sweet song, a man's voice picked up the tune as Alice passed – something nostalgic about love won or lost.

In spite of the hardships, she began to be somewhat reconciled to her daily skirmish with the cold weather and endured it with a degree of good cheer.

In the coldest months Alice closed up most of the large house and they retreated to the kitchen where the stove brought them a modicum of warmth. She was reluctant to venture out into the icy weather to fetch water, but it had to be done. She soon learned that midday, when the weak sun struggled through the blanketing cloud, was the best time to bring in enough water to last twenty-four hours.

She began to attend Sunday services at the small stone church across the way and found a modicum of tranquility in the old almost-forgotten words and chants. She felt comforted by the blessings given to the congregation by the fair-haired priest:

Benedìcat vos omnipotens Deus,
Pater, et Filius,
et Spìritus Sanctus. Amen.

The chapel

At first, it had been hard. Alice was used to American luxuries; running water, electricity and a flushing toilet. But this was what war did to people, she thought, it made them adjust and adapt.

In America, she had shopped at a local supermarket. In Paron, she got used to the idea of a local market where once a week outlying farmers brought their produce for sale. At first she was amused as she watched the farmers and their wives walk in to Paron wearing sabots. Then they removed their sabots and carefully hid them under a hedge, replacing them with their smart leather shoes and walked the rest of the way into the village center. Obviously, it would not do to be seen in wooden clogs. Things changed later, of course, when only two pairs of shoes per person were allowed and everyone wore sabots.

Alice bought what she could at the once-a-week market. What she could not buy there, she bought at the small grocery store in Sens. She could afford very little as Emile's army pay did not amount to much. But it was enough and, in those early days, she managed fairly well.

Learning how to care for her baby was another adventure. When six-month-old Evelyne cried, Alice wrapped her up and took her outside to the garden pump; baby tucked under one arm and the bucket dangling from the other.

"Sur le pont d'Avignon, l'on y danse, l'on y danse," she sang to Evelyne. *"Sur le pont d'Avignon, l'on y danse tout en rond."*

On the last line she would swing Evelyne high into the air, delighting in the baby's chuckles.

Alice was in awe of the miracle of birth, the gift of this beautiful little being to her and Emile. She had not thought of her *Maman* for a long time but now, having a child of her own, brought into vivid focus her mother's ravaged face, the stale smell of her last illness and the slow hoarse cough that seemed to echo through the small rooms where they lived. How her mother must have suffered at the thought of leaving her three children, so young and vulnerable. Alice could not remember her father. He was just a shadowy figure like a silhouette on the wall created by a flickering fire.

And here she was with a child of her own. In spite of the hard work and loneliness, the outside world retreated when she lay on the mattress in front of the stove and watched Evelyne sleeping, her soft curls catching the light of the glowing coals. Nothing mattered, only this child.

All it needed now was for Emile to share this joy. He would be home soon, his letters were full of that promise and, in the meantime, the fire would not make itself and water would not magically appear in the sink.

Early one morning when Alice had, for the second time, wiped off the starry frost from the inside of the windows, Louise Fromont arrived at her door.

"Come along, Alice," she said. "The Jochmans have invited us to visit."

Louise marched purposefully up to the Jochmans' farm gate dragging a reluctant Alice behind her. When she had first arrived in Paron Louise, being one who introduced herself to anyone she thought would benefit her, had rapidly become acquainted with the Jochmans family. They were landowners, people of substance, therefore worth knowing. It would be a pleasure to converse sedately with moneyed people. It was, after all, no more than her due.

Louise made it clear to all who would listen that she was pleased to be back in France and considered all the talk of war pure nonsense. She had long ago decided not to concern herself with something that, in her mind, would not happen.

"I shall convince them not to fear the Germans just as I have convinced any number of my friends," she said. "I am an American and I say there will be no war. It's very possible the Jochmans will disagree with me. But I shall make it my duty to dissuade them."

"I think your argument will fall on deaf ears, *tante*," Alice murmured. "You told me they lived in Belgium and lost everything during the Great War. They know what it will be like if the Germans invade France."

"Germans? Invasion? Nonsense! They won't. They wouldn't dare. France has the finest army in Europe. Don't argue with me, Alice. I know what I know."

She pushed open the farm gate and stomped up the path to the Jochmans' front door.

Alice loved the Jochmans farm. For her, it was the epitome of France and what was really important in life. A grape vine clambered over the porch and nearby some hens scratched in the hard ground. Beyond the solid brick house a few pigs lay, plump and content in the watery rays of the winter sun, and behind the house the stables looked solid and comfortable.

Louise knocked imperiously on the open door and marched across the threshold. A small girl, her hair hanging in pigtails, stared curiously at them. A boy joined her and together they crowded round, talking in high-pitched voices, like quarrelsome birds.

A thin smile barely reached Louise's eyes as she backed away from the children. She had once told Alice that children were a nuisance with their bawling dependence and constant need for attention. It seemed that her very stance radiated dislike and Alice noted the two children, wise beyond their years as children often are, were not taken in by Louise's lackluster attempt at affability.

When they saw Evelyne they chucked the baby under her chin and begged to hold her. They took hold of Alice's hand and pulled her into the kitchen, calling to their mother that there were visitors and one had a baby.

The large kitchen seemed to pulse with energetic life. There was Emilienne, the eldest and about eight-years-old and Ferdinand, a little older; bouncing, chatting, laughing. The baby Therese, the same age as Evelyne, was cradled on her mother's hip. Alice felt comforted. Here was a woman who knew the motherhood ropes, someone to whom she could turn for advice. Godelieve Jochmans gave her an understanding smile.

Alice thought she and Godelieve could become friends; after all, they both had babies and they both had husbands with the name Emile. It seemed a good omen.

Later when the children's interest in the visitors had abated and Alice and her aunt were seated at the table, Godelieve answered Alice's many questions. Yes, there was only her Emile to run the farm with what help she could give, in between running the house and looking after the children. There were so few able-bodied men left in Paron that women had to shoulder as many of the burdens as they could.

Fifty percent of the men of Paron had died in the Great War, Godelieve said, it was probably the same in villages throughout France. The men who had returned were often damaged and disfigured, shell-shocked and with lungs ruined by mustard gas. They were of little use to the farmers. If you walked down the streets of Paron you saw them, sitting in patches of sun, coughing and hunched. It was hard to forget the Great War when you were reminded daily of its consequences. She was just grateful, Godelieve said, that her own dear Emile was still with her, a Belgian native and victim of the Germans in the Great War. He was too old for active service, she said with relief.

The kitchen was filled with the aroma of beef casserole and vegetables. The children ran underfoot, playing catch and giggling while their *Maman* stirred something fragrant on the stove. This is a typical French family, Alice thought. I want this for my child; a loving, vocal, busy household with loads of children and *Maman* clearly the lynch-pin around which the family joyfully revolved.

M. Jochmans entered the kitchen and threw his coat over the back of a chair. Emilienne and Ferdinand crowded around chattering and pointing to their visitors.

"*Bonjour*, Mme Fromont *et* Mme Pothron, *la femme* of the brave axe-wielding Emile."

He was a heavily-built man with broad shoulders and muscled arms. He stretched out a large weathered hand that would look at home on a plough handle. His smile was warm.

"And this is Mademoiselle Evelyne Claudette."

He took Evelyne into his arms and tickled her under her chin. She grabbed hold of his finger and bit on it. Emile Jochmans laughed, tore off the hard end of a baguette and offered it to her. Evelyne gurgled her approval.

Godelieve brought tureens of casserole and vegetables to the table. There was also warm crusty bread, salted butter and homemade sausage on earthenware plates. Little was said as the food disappeared. Finally, M. Jochmans contemplated his empty coffee mug. Then he spoke from the heart, his words solemn and his audience silent.

"These are sad times. As you know the Germans are sweeping through Europe and are likely to invade

France at any time. We don't know what is happening. Our government, our newspapers, our radio – no one tells us the truth. Even our churchmen are beating around the bush, not knowing what to say. We hear wild rumors and nobody knows what to believe. We can only base our knowledge on what happened when the Germans invaded Belgium and France in the last war."

"We should be back in America," grumbled Alice. "We shouldn't be here at all."

"So Louise has told us," M. Jochmans said smiling. "You seem to have got caught up in something that is no longer your affair. Nevertheless, you are here and it was my pleasure to have met your fine husband, even in such amusing circumstances."

Louise looked questioningly at Emile Jochmans.

"Has Alice not told you about the pig?" he asked. "Never mind. Later perhaps." He turned back to Alice and winked. "But more to the point. We were in Belgium during the last war. We came to France in 1925, but before that we were wiped out by the Germans. Our farm was destroyed. We lost everything."

"But they won't invade France, will they?" Alice wanted to stick stubbornly to the possibility that the Germans, satisfied with conquering the rest of Europe, would leave France alone.

"I see no reason why not."

"But what about the Maginot Line? Everyone says it's going to stop them."

"I'm afraid 'everyone' will be proved wrong. Nothing will stop the German Army. Look how it has swept through the rest of Europe. Why would they stop at the Maginot Line? So, I say – when they come," said Emile Jochmans, his voice heavy with foreboding. "They will be like summer locusts and they will mow down everything in their path. Now, we have a farm near Charny that the Germans won't find. It's up in the hills and they won't go there."

"Why not?"

M. Jochmans smiled. "They'll only go where their vehicles can take them. The mountains of France will always be safe. Besides, fighting men do not like facing an enemy above them. It is bad strategy. Of course, they might decide to stop at the French border but there's no reason to believe they will. So, I have made some plans. When the time comes I intend to take the rest of our livestock and farm implements and go to Charny. We'll close up the house and stay there until things settle down and we know it's safe to return to Paron. We're asking if you and your child would like to go with us."

"If we go then how will my husband find us?"

Alice missed the small glance that passed between Emile and Godelieve Jochmans. They remembered the wholesale slaughter of young men only twenty years ago and the many who did not return to their wives.

"We'll find a way to let him know," M. Jochmans said soothingly. "We can't leave you here, our hearts won't allow it. We'll be taking other women and children with us and you are very welcome to come along too."

"But Emile said we'd be safe here," Alice protested.

"Yes, I agree," Louise said. "We are Americans. Nothing will happen to us."

"Exactly," Alice said. "America isn't fighting this war. Mr. Roosevelt has said so. We're neutral. We still have our passports and the Germans will respect them, I'm sure."

M. Jochmans shrugged. "I think you should keep your nationality to yourself for the time being. It is possible they will intern foreign aliens and that might mean you and your child will have to go into a camp."

"I don't know, I just don't know what to do," Alice said.

November nights were clear and through the star-sharp sky Alice sent passionate prayers to God that Emile would soon be home and there would be no decision to make. She was prepared to bargain with the God of her understanding, to hedge her bets and prayed equally fervently to the harsh, judgmental God of the orphanage and the tender more loving God she personally believed in. She gave instructions, pleaded and wept. Finally she decided that whoever was in charge of the world would send Emile home at the right time and they would be reunited.

If anything, December was colder than the month before. Snow fell in ever-increasing fury, carpeting the garden and creating ice patterns on the tiles around the water pump. Trees cracked and broke under the weight of snow. A white wall banked up against the house and along the road men and women slipped and slithered on black ice when the snow turned to rain and the rain froze, slick as windows.

On Christmas Day the weather cleared suddenly and patches of sunlight reflected like tiny mirrors on the snow. Alice placed Evelyne in the stroller and walked to Mass in the little chapel over the road. The familiar scent of incense, the mumbled responses and the joyful singing of Christmas hymns was a source of great comfort.

After Mass she went to a late Christmas lunch with Louise and Jules. Alice was still a little wary of her uncle. In New York he had abused his position and had tried to grope her whenever she was alone with him. If only Louise knew, Alice thought. Or perhaps she did, as very little escaped her aunt. Jules was older now and his appetite for young girls might have faded. Nevertheless Alice kept as far from him as possible, fearing a snaking lascivious hand when she least expected it. Being in the same room as Jules Duxin had always been a rather chilling affair.

In spite of this, Alice continued to feel at home in Paron. There was an air of peace and tranquility in the hills and the hawthorn hedges, in the river where voices seemed to speak among the rustling reeds and from the old stone cottages that marched up from the river bank. There was a sense of earthy wisdom in the faces of the black-clad neighbors, some of whom were beginning to greet her with a smile or a wave. And some evenings when the air was still Alice thought she could hear the chapel choir practicing in the big church in Sens, their voices floating across the river like feathers.

Emile's letters, censored with thick black lines, told of a waiting game. The phony war continued with German troops staring across their Siegfried Line and the French naively assuming their safety within the fortress of the Maginot Line. Political intrigue continued but the general population was not privy to decisions made on their behalf. Instead people battled on in ignorance, with the seemingly never-ending cold and the growing shortages of food and clothing.

The old year ended and 1940 stole in like a thief in the night. And still the cold persisted. In January there was little food in the store and Alice began to be increasingly imaginative about what she could buy and how to cook it. The Jochmans helped where they could but even they were beginning to tighten their belts. Alice was happy to make sacrifices. She thought of Emile and imagined the food that should be on her plate going to him instead. The thought cheered her up considerably as she pushed the rickety old stroller across the bridge to Sens and to the nearest grocery store.

Alice paused outside *de l'épiciere* in Sens and looked through the store window at the clear-swept sawdust on the floor, the rows of barrels that should have been heaped with grain, dried peas, sugar and flour, but were now almost empty. To one side were large round glass jars with only the sticky residue of brightly colored candy. Behind the high counter wooden shelves lined the walls and held a steadily dwindling stock of imported food items; sugar, tea, coffee, rice. At the back she could dimly make out the gaunt figure of *Mme La Commerçante*. Alice wondered where Monsieur Grocer had got to. Was he perhaps one of the men who had not come back from the Great War? Since 1918 so many businesses were being run by women. They had no voting power but were in control of the everyday affairs of the nation – those that mattered. Alice felt a sturdy pride as she watched *Mme La Commerçante* serve a customer. Here was a woman on her own, running a food store. Not bad, Alice thought.

"*Bonjour,* Madame Pothron," a voice called out from along the street.

The woman was older than Alice and under her swinging coat she wore a red silk dress, fashionably gathered into a flounce on the hip. Her auburn hair was bouffant in the latest Paris-fashion, piled into a great sweep on the top of her head and held with tortoise-shell combs. She was beautifully made up, mascara, lipstick and rouge on her cheekbones. Alice felt quite mousy beside this rather elegant creature.

"*Je m'appelle* Lulu," the woman said, clasping Alice's hands, her breath sending a warm cloud into the cold morning air. "My name is really Lucienne but everyone calls me Lulu. So much easier, don't you think? I have a place of work here in Sens."

A businesswoman, Alice thought, how elegant. "What is your work, Madame?" Alice asked.

"They haven't told you yet?" Lulu laughed. "You're going to buy food from the old cow?"

"*Oui*, I have no choice." Alice gazed through the store window and saw a look of horror slowly engulf Madame Grocer's face. She wondered why.

"She cheats," Lulu said.

Alice grinned. "Yes, I know."

"Are you alone? No husband?"

Alice gave a noncommittal shrug.

"Ah, I understand. He is away. You are *l'Américaine?*"

"*Oui.*"

Lulu slipped her arm through Alice's and gently guided her away from the store window. Alice could smell the piney scent of clean hair as the woman whispered in her ear. "Well, don't tell anyone. We won't know for a while who we can trust and even whispers can be dangerous."

"But how did you know?"

"Jules Duxin told me," Lulu said. "We'll speak again, Alice Pothron." She waved a set of lacquered fingernails in Alice's direction as she strode away.

Alice walked thoughtfully into *l'épicierie*. It smelt of apples.

Behind the counter the woman was stony-faced. "You are new here, Madame?" she asked. "If I were you I would choose my friends a little more carefully. That woman is a *prostituée.*"

A prostitute? Oh Lord, thought Alice, stifling a small bubble of laughter. The only woman in Sens to stop and speak to her and it was the local whore. What was the world coming to? A good thing she could see the funny side.

"Thank you for your concern, Madame," she said as calmly as she could. "But I will choose my own friends."

Madame Grocer's face was rigid with disapproval. It could have been the countrywoman's natural reticence of a stranger who wore different clothes and affected strange airs. One who never wore black even though rumor had it her husband was a soldier fighting for France. Or perhaps the grocer's spite was for someone who was fussy about the age of the grain she sold and who noticed the lead washer stuck to the underside of the scale. Or was it only that this strange little woman who said she was from Paris had spoken in a friendly way to the local prostitute? Whatever it was, Alice faced a stormy cloud of disapproval.

So, the beautiful woman was a prostitute. Alice thought about it on the way home. And Jules had told her about his niece being an American. Alice put two and two together and grinned. Dirty old man, she thought.

But, on a more serious note, Lulu was the second person in a few days who had warned her to keep her nationality a secret. What did they know that she did not?

CHAPTER 7

Stand not upon the order of your going,
But go at once.
- William Shakespeare

Military thinking of the time was still dominated by the *attaque a l'outrance* or the all-out frontal charge with a huge loss of human life. It was the traditional way of waging war. It had worked for centuries and nothing was likely to change. Was it?

Brigadier General Charles de Gaulle was almost alone in predicting changes to the way wars would be conducted. In 1934 he published a book, *The Army of the Future*, in which he foresaw a mechanized army capable of swift attack and defended by a disciplined air force. Sadly, the only person to take the message to heart was Adolf Hitler, whose army would eventually advance at an incredible forty miles an hour. The attack on Europe, when it came, was not named *Blitzkreig* or 'lightning war' for nothing.

France's government was ripe for defeat. Made up of yesterday's men, there were no new ideas, no courage, no certainty, only timidity and vacillation. The French had long since lost respect for their government filled with quarrelsome old men who would in a few short months give their country away to the enemy. One might say that France was brought to its knees by the petty antagonisms and indecisiveness of its aged leaders.

The Prime Minister, Paul Reynaud, distraught and exhausted, had only taken office in March, a little over two months before the invasion. He had not yet settled in to the role nor had he gathered allies around him. His position was precarious. He was also hampered in his decision-making by his mistress, the Countess Hélène de Portes, who was quite openly pro-Nazi. Charles de Gaulle, who had led one of the few successful armored counter-attacks on the Germans and who later went on to lead the Free French from London, expressed his disgust when he said the Prime Minister's office had been turned into a "petticoat mockery".

On Friday 10 May 1940, nine months after the declaration of war, Germany began its western offensive. Very early on the same morning the first air raid sirens in Paris wailed their ominous message.

Emile and the other medics at the *Ecurie* at Versailles listened to the radio as the Minister of Propaganda, Ludovic-Oscar Frossard, announced that the phony war was over and hostilities had begun. Emile felt a shudder of apprehension. As a medical team they would be sent to the frontline, wherever that was. If the Great War was anything to go by then his life expectancy on the front would be about six weeks. He felt sick.

By Monday 13 May, the German Army had cut its way through the defenses of Belgium, Holland and Luxembourg and was heading for France. Then, to the utter horror of the French, German Panzer divisions, supported by the Luftwaffe, bypassed the Maginot Line and entered France through the Ardennes Forest and over the River Meuse north of the Maginot Line. This was not supposed to happen.

Alice sat in the living room with her aunt and uncle discussing the latest news. The impregnable

Maginot Line had proved to be a three billion franc fantasy. Nothing was going to stop the enemy. They would soon be everywhere. Louise sobbed loudly, afraid at last.

Once the enemy had entered French territory the population's facade of naivety and good cheer vanished and panic set in. Residents of Reims in northern France were the first to join the refugees from the Low Countries who had spilled over the border and were clogging the roads. Soon the roads to the south were congested with terrified scrambling hordes of refugees. When the order came from French Army commanders – 'every man for himself' – soldiers threw down their weapons and fled, joining the hysteria on the roads.

Alice woke up on the morning of Wednesday 15 May with someone hammering on her door. She groaned, shoved her feet into her shoes and hobbled, disheveled and half-drunk with sleep, to the window.

"You must get out, Madame," shrieked her neighbor, Mme Faure. "I've just heard the Germans are slaughtering women and children. There are parachutists landing just south of Reims. They're coming through the cornfields, Madame, *les torses nus*. I heard it on the radio."

"Now, don't take on so, Madame. It's just a rumor!"

"No, it's true! The newspaper headlines say that fifth columnists in Paris are going around disguised as nuns."

It can't be true. Bare-chested soldiers? Men disguised as nuns?

It was then she looked up and stared with horror at the mass of exhausted people moving slowly over the bridge from Sens. It had been a trickle a few days ago. Now it was like a flooded river, incoherent and chaotic.

On Thursday 16 May, as the Germans advanced on Paris, government ministers fled south to the Chateaux of the Loire valley. Restless and unnerved they moved on to Tours, then to Bordeaux and finally settled in Vichy, a small health-spa town from where 'free' France would be governed.

By Monday 20 May, the Germans had established Panzer corridors to the coast, driving the Allied troops to the Channel. Between Sunday 26 May and Monday 3 June – just one week – 198,000 men of the British Expeditionary Force and 140,000 French, Belgian and Dutch soldiers were evacuated from the beaches of Dunkirk by English boats of all shapes and sizes. Two French divisions were ordered to remain in order to protect the evacuation and only 40,000 French soldiers from this particular fiasco finally fell into German hands or escaped and went home. These brave Frenchmen rose to the occasion and helped avoid a total disaster at Dunkirk.

The French Army fought with great courage in the six weeks after the German Panzers crashed through the border and into France. One hundred and thirty thousand Frenchmen died in the hopeless, leaderless defense of France, more than twice the number of American casualties at Normandy in 1944.

The mood in Paris and other towns and cities had generally been good as long as officials went on pretending that France could be saved. Media reports, both newspaper and radio, had been unwholesomely optimistic, relaying false or biased news of French victories and breezy predictions about the magnificent French Army that was, even then, in full flight. The bubble burst when the oil depots at Port Jerome near Rouen were sabotaged by locals who did not want valuable fuel to fall into German hands. When an oily haze hung on the horizon people in Paris finally began to think about evacuation.

On Monday 3 June, Paris suffered its first air raid when the Luftwaffe targeted the airports. Orly, Villacoublay and Le Bourget were destroyed as well as factories in the 15th and 16th *arondissements* or districts. More than two hundred people were reported killed.

After waiting a week for some kind of instruction, Captain Delavierre went to Army headquarters in central Paris to find someone, anyone, who would order the evacuation of the Medical units from Versailles. On his return Delavierre marshaled the men into the cobbled courtyard. They were restless and apprehensive, looking to him for a reassurance he could not give.

"Buses have been parked across the streets to stop airplanes from landing," he told his men as they gathered round for the latest news. "That'll also frustrate any German mechanized divisions."

"Just give us the leaders and we'll follow them into hell," someone shouted and the others murmured in agreement. Delavierre knew the ordinary soldier would do just that, but there were no leaders and there were no plans. At military headquarters all he had found was abandoned filing cabinets and smoldering heaps of files in the gardens.

"Are the Germans bombing the city?"

"Not yet," he said. "But the authorities have sandbagged most of the major buildings so bombing is expected."

"But the treasures have gone, haven't they?"

"Yes, I heard that museums and art galleries had packed up all the main treasures and shipped them out of the city and to the south. It was all done months ago."

"The Louvre as well?"

"*Oui.*"

"But where to?"

Delavierre shrugged. "Who knows? To various Châteaux, I should think. No one's talking but I heard it whispered that the Winged Victory of Samothrace from the Louvre had gone to the *Château de Valençay* in the Loire valley. Rumors, of course. They wouldn't want the Germans to know. Anyway, they don't need to bomb Paris. I can tell you now; there'll be no defense of the city. It's practically empty."

"I heard you can still buy a glass of wine and a packet of Gauloises."

One of the men laughed. "The day we can't buy French cigarettes is the day we die!"

"Did you see any of the damage, *mon capitaine?*"

"*Non,* but I was told the airports have gone."

"And what do we do now?"

Delavierre shrugged. "Wait, I suppose, until we're told what to do."

At the *Ècurie* they were still getting used to the sirens that howled each night, filling the air with menace. The faint whistle and then the whine of the sirens was the signal for orderlies to scurry around checking shutters and blackout curtains. Sometimes they heard the crump of bombs further north or the low drone as the Luftwaffe sought new targets. Patients would mumble sleepily "*qu'est-ce que c'est?*" What is it? Then the orderly on duty would take his torch and walk up and down the wards quietly comforting the fearful. A touch on the shoulder, a whisper was all it needed. Those too sick and the dying did not care, but most of the men were restless and afraid. They lay rigid and vulnerable in their beds. Soon the three-tone signal reassured them the danger was over. They could turn over and go back to sleep.

Then in the northern suburbs of Paris, the Basse Seine oil storage depot was sabotaged. Oily smoke hung over the city like a mourner's veil. This was the moment when Parisians fully understood the enormity of what was about to occur. The German army would soon be in Paris.

It was as if the dynamiting of the depot was the signal that energized the people of Paris, wound them up like toys and set them jolting along the roads. In all, between six and ten million people – about a quarter of the population – left their homes throughout the northern part of France and clogged the roads south, west and east, carrying whatever they could, going wherever they thought it would be safe. There was nothing orderly about 'the order of their going'. Nothing mattered, only the animal instinct to flee.

By the time the Germans entered Paris on 14 June 1940, it was almost a ghost town. Shutters were closed, shops and offices boarded up and the streets silent. Those who had remained watched warily from behind lace curtains or stood in the streets, tears pouring down their faces. The conquerors had not expected a fanfare of welcome but they had not expected the silent streets either.

On this lovely day in June it seemed as if Paris was holding its breath.

First to arrive on the Champs-Elysées were the motorcyclists in leather overcoats and coal bucket helmets, followed by dark green vehicles bristling with men and weapons. Then arrogant men on horseback (even their mounts seemed to be aware of the occasion as they pranced and postured down the

Champs-Elysées). Lastly long columns of foot soldiers marching, row upon row, solemn and proud with their red and black flags whipping in the breeze. They had much to be proud of. In a few short months they had conquered the whole of Europe.

Soon the swastika – the "burning red flags with the white circle and the black spider in the middle" as Arthur Koestler described it – flew everywhere as the Germans made themselves at home. They were determined to make a good impression, as Hitler had commanded. The young soldiers, tall, blond, clean and neatly dressed, set out to win over the French population, not oppress them.

That would come later.

In towns and cities across France, *gendarmes* stuck big red placards on walls announcing that all enemy aliens were to be interned in *camps de concentration*. Jules saw the notice in Sens and hurried home. There was a heated discussion with Alice and Louise as to whether they would be considered 'enemy aliens'.

"We're Americans," Louise said. "We're neutral."

"Don't be stupid, Louise," Jules hissed. "Anyone who isn't one of them will be suspect." He turned to Alice. "I hope you haven't told anyone here that you're American."

"No, *oncle*. Who would I tell?"

"That prostitute friend of yours for one," Jules said. He must have seen the look on Alice's face for he hurried on. "Anyway, it probably means Jews and communists. And trade unionists. People like that, not us. We are foreign aliens, not enemy aliens. There's a difference and I'm sure the Germans will respect that."

"We have our *carte d'identité*," Louise said. "We can pass for French."

The others nodded.

On the 16 June 1940, two days after Paris was taken, Reynaud resigned rather than conclude an armistice with Germany. The 84 year-old hero of World War I, Philippe Pétain, took over leadership. He would have no such qualms.

Pétain believed the world as he knew it had come to an end as, indeed, it had. France was defeated and Pétain smugly imagined the defeat of Britain would soon follow and when that happened Germany would prevail over the whole world. He saw no point in fighting and bringing down the wrath of the mighty Wehrmacht onto the people of France.

When the dust had settled, Germany occupied three-fifths of the country (the more populated northern area with greater resources) and Pétain agreed to an armistice wherein France would pay the financial cost of occupation. At four hundred million francs a day it was a figure that would eventually cripple France's ability to survive.

Within a few short months the French population would realize that, for all his past glory and his plans for a 'new' France, Pétain had become Hitler's stooge. Worse, within the year he would ask the people of France to collaborate with the Nazis.

In order to maintain the myth that the French people were being headed by a civilian government, albeit an authoritarian dictatorship, Pétain and his compliant cronies were allowed by the Germans to function from Vichy. This unelected government had draconian powers over the civilian population. Using Vichy to further their oppressive program meant the Germans were insulating themselves from discontent and maintaining a façade of peaceful co-operation.

Only five days after taking office Pétain enacted the first anti-Semitic legislation, the infamous *Statut des Juifs.* It was far more stringent than Germany's own anti-Jewish laws. Later the Vichy government would hand over to the Germans not only foreign-born Jews who had arrived as refugees but also French citizens who were Jewish. These people were sent to concentration camps and then to their deaths.

In so doing Pétain and his cronies betrayed the honor of France.

CHAPTER 8

Around them, behind them, in front of them,
people were fleeing. Occasionally the road rose more
steeply and they could see clearly the chaotic
multitude trudging through the dust, stretching far
into the distance.

- Irène Némirovsky

As the Germans swept into the capital city the
roads south of Paris were clogged with frightened
refugees, some of whom had travelled from Belgium
and Holland and were fleeing just ahead of the
ravenous jaws of the *Wehrmacht*.

On the first day, tattered lines of refugees had
reached far into the countryside. Meadows and
regimented vineyards surrounded them as they
trudged through the dappled shade of the poplar
trees that lined the road. It was a warm summer's
day, birds sang from the hedgerows and a gentle
breeze combed the grass verges. By midday the heat
was oppressive but the lines of weary people kept
coming, row upon row.

Those who crowded the roads were exhausted.
They were hungry and thirsty. In their precipitous
flight few had given thought to food or water. They
had assumed there would be stores, hotels, bistros
and restaurants along the way. There was nothing
but the endless green of the vineyards and fields.

Their exodus had been sudden. Most had no idea
where they were going or what lay in store. The
Loire, ninety miles south of Paris, seemed their best

prospect. Beyond that they would surely be out of harm's way. It was the shining hope of the river that gave them the strength to go on.

Those who were not exhausted appreciated the peace and tranquility through which they were walking. So different from the bustle and noise of Paris, the Metro, the buses, the stores full of manufactured goods. Here the sound of bees, the flight of strange birds and the perfume of hedgerows and tilled earth lulled them into a false sense of peace.

When the first attack came, it took them by surprise.

It came out of nowhere and at treetop height. German Stukas swept down on them like enraged wasps, sirens shrieking and machine guns spurting into the human tide. Bullets ripped the air like torn silk. People scattered into the ditches and behind trees. Mothers covered their children; some shocked into silence, others screaming.

When the grey Stukas left the refugees picked themselves up and walked on, leaving the dead, leaving their luggage, leaving their terror in the ditches and behind the trees; taking with them only their knowledge of this new horror.

A loud drone and once more they plunged towards the ditches, hiding wherever they could as a second wave of Stukas yelped and whined like a pack of dogs leaping on the defenseless columns.

By 13 June, Captain Delavierre had still not received any orders. He had phoned and telegraphed anyone who might know, but all he heard were rumors. It was obvious that there would be no instructions from Headquarters and Delavierre was on his own. Belatedly, he gathered the Fifth Medical

Section on to the parade ground and spoke to his men. They seemed to sense his unease and stood erect and edgy as he gave his orders. He had made a unilateral and unofficial decision to evacuate his men and the wounded and sick under their care. He would take them and go south with as much of the medical equipment as they could pack into the ambulances. He had heard that General Weygand, Supreme Commander of the French Army, had set up headquarters at Briare at the *Chateau de Mugue* across the Loire where he would re-assemble his scattered forces. It seemed the obvious place for Delavierre to take his unit. A three-hour journey at the most. They would be there for lunch.

The unit hurriedly gathered the walking wounded into canvas-covered trucks. The more seriously ill and injured were taken on stretchers and gently loaded into waiting ambulances. Another truck was loaded with medical equipment and medicines. Delavierre ordered his men to destroy everything that remained. Emile took a hammer and demolished his x-ray machines.

They drove south, with Delavierre in the lead ambulance, and quickly became part of *l'exode*. They joined mile after dreadful mile of marching people who were stolid with exhaustion and desolation. Children were lost and sometimes found. Old people sat on the side of the road, unable to go further. Furniture, pets, clothing were abandoned. Among the walking crowd were hundreds of soldiers still in uniform, unarmed, ragged, leaderless, their shoulders hunched. The message was in their hopeless eyes and in their dragging feet.

France had been defeated.

It was almost dark before Delavierre saw the river. He guided them out of the chaos and into a side street. Shuttered houses loomed dark and empty on either side of the road. Stray dogs scattered as they approached. Although only a distance of ninety-three miles, it had taken them almost a day to get to the Loire. But they were ahead of the invaders and that was all that mattered.

The drivers made their slow way towards the bridge that would take them south of the river. But they were in for a shock. The bridges spanning the Loire River at Gien had been blown up and lay in crushed heaps of rubble along the river banks.

The men groaned. There seemed to be no way they could get across. Captain Delavierre signaled the way forward. The rest followed as he slowly drove away from the town until they came to a small village on the bank of the turgid river. There the bridge was also in ruins but they stopped for the night, exhausted, hungry and depressed at the sights they had witnessed. Around them the fields seemed as empty as the houses; no cattle, no birds flying overhead. Only small wild creatures scurried to safety as the angry sun set behind a bank of feathered cloud.

The men tended to the wounded, handed out water and morphine, changed bandages and adjusted splints. Some rooted around in the nearby gardens looking for something to eat. Emile walked past the shuttered houses, past the gates swinging on rusty hinges. Finally he came to a small cemetery. A row of new graves caught his attention. Hastily dug, a few had crosses marked with a name but more often just a message; unknown woman, aged forty, blonde hair; a boy ten years and a girl, about six months, found together; an old woman with a cameo brooch. Shaken, he hurried back to his division.

"The bombing of the bridges is the work of the Luftwaffe," one soldier groaned. "The Germans must be ahead of us."

Another, more hopeful. "Perhaps our boys did it."

Someone responded eagerly. "Maybe they're finally going to make a stand."

"It has to be. The river is the natural barrier."

"It's possible the French High Command has the Army settling in," Delavierre said. "We'll know more in the morning."

"Perhaps we can use a pontoon to get across."

"It's dangerous. We could be shot at."

"*Oui*, by our own chaps," was someone's gloomy reply.

"We'll get across tomorrow one way or another," Delavierre said reassuringly. "Settle down now, we need to sleep."

The men lay down wherever they could find a level place, muttering among themselves, mulling over what they'd seen on the road from Paris. Emile was not alone in his disappointment at the behavior of some of the men and women. It seemed as if terror had turned many into wild animals fighting for survival. As for the German Stukas, someone said, you couldn't expect anything better from such barbarians, slaughtering innocent civilians. But Emile wondered if the enemy was actually targeting the men in uniform walking with the civilians. It was hard to know. He felt physically sick and was no longer sure if it was hunger or something more corrosive. He lay down to sleep, using his coat as a pillow. It was a long time before the images faded.

In the morning, they found one of their patients had died. They gently lifted him out of the ambulance and left him on the side of the road. Again, a few men foraged in the gardens and brought back some apples and ripe tomatoes which they shared. Delavierre regretted he had not thought about including a mobile kitchen in his convoy. It had not seemed necessary at the time, Briare was so close. They should have arrived there by lunchtime yesterday. He had not calculated on the roads being clogged with fleeing Parisians and that the journey would take almost three times as long.

He went to each ambulance and checked on the patients. Several were well enough to sit up. He did what he could to alleviate the suffering of those who were worse. One young man was crying with pain. Delavierre gave him morphine and sat at his side until the man became quiet and finally fell asleep.

The peace of the morning was soon shattered. The Luftwaffe's bombers ripped at the air, rocking the ground. Banks along the river spewed up in geysers of grey mud as the pilots unleashed their bombs, targeting Gien and other towns along the Loire. It seemed to confirm what Delavierre and his men believed – the French Army was going to make a stand south of the river and the Germans were making it as difficult for them as possible.

Later, when the bombers departed, Delavierre and Emile inspected the river. It was less turbulent than in the town, although the bank was a slurry of mud and debris. Emile wondered what his Captain had in mind. He found out soon enough when Delavierre gathered the able-bodied men around him. They passed around the last of their cigarettes and listened to what he had to say.

"We've got to get across the river," he said. "The Germans aren't far behind and we have to get the wounded to safety."

"And ourselves," someone shouted.

"Yes, and ourselves," Delavierre replied.

He ordered the men to search for wood, empty oil barrels and rope. Under his leadership they soon constructed a large, crude pontoon. It took a few hours, much swearing and sweat, many crushed fingers and scraped hands. By noon it was ready. They ferried their ambulances across, then turned back and ferried some of the refugees who had been stranded in Gien and had followed them west. They poled back and forth, ferrying as many refugees as they could before leaving the pontoon in the hands of some able-bodied men to continue their flight to Briare.

They scrambled back into the ambulances and drove on, watching all the while for the return of the enemy planes. The men were calm, but whether it was the calm of resignation Emile could not tell. It was a forlorn hope that the invasion would stop at the Loire. It certainly looked a likely place for the French Army to regroup and finally face the Germans instead of running away. The destruction of the bridges could mean the Army had finally turned round and was preparing to fight. But Emile was not so sure. In spite of the courage and panache of the average soldier, even he knew the Army hierarchy had shown little courage or determination to face the enemy and continue the battle.

"Do you think we'll be safe when we get to Briare?" he asked.

Delavierre gave a Gallic shrug, his arms outstretched. "I'm hoping we'll meet up with Weygand and the rest of the Army. Then we'll know."

Emile thought Delavierre looked exhausted. The men were hungry and they had run out of morphine for the patients. Emile realized if they did not get to safety very soon some of the more seriously injured men might die. The journey had been tough on them.

The road along the south bank of the Loire was not as crowded as the Paris to Gien road. It ran east along the river, through small villages, a field or two of grain then in and out of a dark forest. In the shade of the trees it was deliciously cool with the dying sunlight occasionally piercing through the dappled shadow. Fellow travelers also seemed to feel the peace of the surrounding trees as they walked, with more purpose and less panic, towards Briare.

But it was too good to last and the end, when it came, was sudden.

They rounded a corner of the forest road moving slowly to cushion the injured in the ambulances. A fallen tree had been pulled across the road to act as a barrier. Behind it stood the enemy, machine guns pointing down the road, rifles at the ready. A German officer waved them to a stop.

"Halt!" He shouted. "Paris has surrendered. It's all over. For you the war is over."

For Emile and the medical corps in which he served, the war was indeed over. He sat with the others from his unit on the side of the road and dully accepted cigarettes from the grinning enemy soldiers.

Questions tumbled around in his mind. How could Paris have fallen so quickly? How could magnificent French Army have been overwhelmed without even putting up a decent fight? Why had the Maginot Line, the fortress they had been told was impregnable, not protected France from the Germans? How could it be over in less than six weeks?

It was obvious even to Emile, a relative stranger to French politics, that the government's failure to lead and provide stability largely contributed to the chaos. The tentativeness of France's leaders had been one of the main causes of the breakdown of civil and military order and discipline, as Emile and the rest of the Medical Unit had witnessed on the roads south of Paris.

Disheartened, dirty and hungry they were returned the next day to Paris under German escort and placed in a makeshift prison at the Val de Grace military hospital in the 5th *arondissement*.

Their German guards prepared them for the worst. They made it quite clear that, because the French soldiers did not show the same kind of bravery as their fathers had in the Great War – which their German enemies had found daunting – they were despised as 'men who had run away'. They could not expect any respect from their captors.

Emile wondered if they had ignored the pleas of the many helpless civilians at Gien and had ferried only their ambulances across the river perhaps they would have been able to outrun the Germans. But it was mere speculation and at least they had done the decent thing.

As the months in the camp dragged by, when they were hungry and dispirited, Emile would try to remember that, when the chips were down, Captain Delavierre and his men had behaved with honor.

CHAPTER 9

Courage is not the absence of fear, but rather
the judgment that something else is more
important than fear.

- Ambrose Redmoon

On Saturday 8 June 1940, Alice celebrated Evelyne's first birthday. There would be no birthday cake, no candles, no party and, as a gift, only a small embroidered dress she had made from an old petticoat.

A few days earlier Evelyne had taken her first chubby teetering steps. Alice had cried for the absent and beloved husband who should have been there to witness the moment. She cried for the country that seemed to be unraveling; for the panicked incoherent people on the roads through Paron, for the America she had left behind and may never see again. In the end, she did not know who or what deserved her tears more.

She needed to stay strong, but it was hard. It astounded her to see how quickly Evelyne picked up her moods and copied her emotions. She constantly made new discoveries about this little person who had entered her life and each day taught her something new. But every discovery was bitter-sweet as there was no Emile with whom to share them. Emile's fate was unknown as there had been no letters, no news. He was somewhere out there, facing God-knew-what challenges and she prayed daily for his wellbeing and safety.

There was a knock on the door and Lulu walked in, a huge smile on her face. Over the months Lulu had become a friend, so Alice was not surprised to see her visit Paron on this particular day.

"*Joyeux anniversaire!*" she called. "Happy birthday, Evelyne! And congratulations to her mother for bringing such a sweet child into the world."

"Oh, Lulu." Alice began to cry again.

Lulu gave her a hug and patted her back in a motherly gesture. She handed Alice a small parcel wrapped in brown paper. Chocolate. Alice had not seen chocolate for months. Together they sat at the kitchen table and broke off chunks, savoring the illicit taste, as bitter-sweet as memory.

Throughout the following two days the refugees continued to march past Alice's front door. They looked exhausted, defeated, lost as they walked slowly through the hot June days and the sultry oppressive nights. As someone said, it was '*la pagaille*' – total chaos.

"Get out, get out while you can," they called when they saw her at the window. "The Germans are coming."

By Tuesday 11 June, something of their desperation finally caught hold of Alice. She stood irresolute, fighting the panic of flight, but finally she was overwhelmed by the fear that was pulsing in through her windows. Where should she go? Of course, Emile had told her to go to Nice.

She began throwing clothes into a suitcase. In a basket she placed bread and cheese, a bottle of milk for Evelyne and Skippy's bone. She locked the side door, hurried down the steps and through the garden. The Citroën Emile had bought stood black and silent in the cobwebbed garage. She shoved the basket and suitcase onto the back seat. Then she loaded a sleepy Evelyne and Skippy into the front.

Outside the throng swept on.

Mon Dieu, she thought. The passports. In her panic she could not remember where Emile had hidden them. She sat on the running board of the auto, her head in her hands.

Think, Alice, think, as the miserable hordes passed by clouding her memory with the stink of their fear. She tried to pinpoint in her mind that last day nine months ago when she and Emile had looked for a suitable hiding place. She looked around the garage, at the rusty garden tools. No, not here. They had thought about it but decided it was too exposed to the street. Then she remembered the attic and their precious passports shoved behind a rough beam in the roof. Alice ran back into the house, up the steps two at a time and felt behind the dusty beam. She pulled out the passports and the money, all the while hearing the slow procession of the doomed and displaced passing her house. She dusted off her hands, went downstairs and prepared herself for the next challenge; driving the Citroën.

She peered at the dashboard. All the knobs and levers looked as they had when Emile drove to Besançon. It felt like a century ago. What were they all for?

Alice felt a rising panic that threatened to engulf her. What had Emile told her? She closed her eyes and brought back the memory of Emile's strong hands. What were they doing? What had they pulled or pushed to get the auto moving?

"Here is the automatic starter. But if that doesn't work, I use the crank handle. I make sure the auto's in neutral when I crank otherwise I'll run over myself," Emile had said. Alice didn't quite know what he meant but logic told her that having the car in gear when she cranked would send the vehicle forward and plaster her against the back wall of the garage.

She had watched him after a fashion and enjoyed listening to his pseudo-lessons in automobile driving. She remembered she had to pull out something on the dashboard and then press the starter button. Or she could take the handle that lay on the floor behind the driver's seat and crank until the engine caught. She pressed the starter button. Nothing. Remembered the choke, pulled it out and tried again. The battery needed more than just the starter to coax it into life. Okay, crank like crazy and hope for the best, she thought. Otherwise, stay at home.

Surprisingly, the Citroën kicked into life with her first effort at cranking. It gave a throaty roar and shuddered invitingly. She threw the crank handle into the back, slid in behind the steering wheel and sat for a moment calming her breathing. Now what?

The gears. Emile had said something about putting your foot on the pedal to get the automobile into gear. But which pedal? There were three. This was harder than she thought.

Evelyne began to cry and Skippy joined in sympathetically. Alice wanted to weep with them but instead she returned to the problem of the pedals. He'd said one was the brake, one was the accelerator and the third one was the gear-changing pedal, whatever that was called. Oh, yes, the clutch. She had one chance in three to get it right.

She pressed the first one and the engine shrieked. Wrong one. 'Second-time-lucky' held for Alice. She slipped the automobile into reverse gear. It shot backwards, scraping against the door frame before she thought to brake. Forward again, slowly with Evelyne crying her offended surprise. Then tentatively backwards with the mudguard loose and banging against the bodywork. The automobile gradually moved out in a fairly straight line and towards the road. She spun the steering wheel, bumped over the curb and turned until she was in the middle of the street. She forced a break in the indignant traffic, changed gear and drove off humpity-bump until she got the hang of it; bicycles, strollers piled high with furniture and weary children, barrows and carts wisely making way for her.

Soon she was caught up in the chaotic tumult on the road.

Women, children, the sick and the elderly trudged southwards carrying what they could. In particular she noted soldiers, haggard and unshaven. They had no officer with them, no orders, no weapons and no hope. The sight of French soldiers, an *armée en déroute* – an army put to flight – and Alice knew the situation was hopeless.

She slowed amid the confusion. A woman banged on the side. Shouted something. The auto surged forward leaving the woman howling her despair in the dust. Evelyne screamed. Skippy cowered, shivering. She moved through a heaving mass of people, panic-stricken and fighting each other for a place. Alice felt caught, swept along by their hysteria.

Toward afternoon, somewhere just north of Auxerre, an awful silence fell upon them. As one they turned and faced north. In the distance they could hear the drone of approaching airplanes. Eyes reddened from dust, fear and fatigue, they saw the sleek grey outlines of planes coming closer until they were above them and at tree height. The air suddenly filled with shrieks as people abandoned their goods and jumped for the ditches. A sound like drumbeats and the planes were so low overhead they could see the pilots grinning as they strafed the helpless and dying. The roar, the smell of blood and cordite, the cries of the wounded were deafening.

As the planes wheeled away men and women struggled to their feet waving their fists at the empty sky and cursing.

"*Merde!*"

"*Fils de pute!*"

"*Fils de salaud!*"

Alice clawed her way up from the ditch into which she and Evelyne had fallen. Near her a man lay dead beside his twisted bicycle, eyes open and a look of surprise on the half of his face that was left. Alice covered Evelyne's eyes and scrambled back into the Citroën. Her mind was made up. Anything had to be better than this awful chaos, this maelstrom of desperate humanity.

She was going home.

She tried to maneuver the Citroën but her foot slithered off the brake and she slammed into an auto ahead of her. Skippy slid off the seat with a squeal, Evelyne on top of him; a tangle of dog and child. No time to check on them as the driver ahead ran up calling, "keep moving, Madame, keep moving." She reversed and tried again. This time she was clear. Going against the tide of traffic, she drove home. It was only then she noticed the floor of the auto was clotted with blood.

At home she allowed her panic to surface. Screaming for someone to help her, Alice picked Evelyne up under one arm and Skippy under the other and ran for the house. Behind her she saw the teenage son of her neighbor.

"Put the car away, Philippe. Put it away," she screamed.

She dragged Evelyne's clothes off; dress, cotton diaper and vest until the child lay naked on the kitchen table. Thank God, she thought. There was no injury, nothing, only some blood stains on her outer garments. Quickly Alice dressed her and then picked Skippy up. His limp body curved in her hands and blood spurted out of a long cut on his side. She put her hand over the cut, stemming the red tide.

Philippe walked into the kitchen. "Madame, here are your auto keys," he said.

"Come quickly. Help me."

"What happened?"

"I don't know. He's cut. Badly. It must have been something on the floor of the auto."

Alice gently placed Skippy on the table, caressing his head as he lay almost comatose.

"Look inside the top drawer of the dresser. See my sewing kit? Bring it here."

Alice grabbed a clean tea towel from one drawer and a bottle of brandy from another.

"What are you doing?" Philippe looked anxious. "Are you a doctor, Madame? A nurse?"

"Neither," said Alice.

She cut away the hair from Skippy's side and wiped the area clean. A long thin line of blood beaded out of the dog's side. Skippy lay slack on the table, dazed and limp. She dashed some of the brandy onto the cut and the dog gave a small protesting whimper.

"Tu-tu," Alice crooned as she threaded a needle and began to sew the wound in Skippy's side.

"Madame, *vous êtes étonnante*," Philippe said.

No, not amazing, Alice thought, just desperate. She felt like telling this young boy, hardly old enough to shave, that when you are forced to confront things you just did the best you could. It was a lesson she was only beginning to learn.

101

A few days later there was a knock on the door. A man in a dirty uniform stood before her, exhausted, his cheeks sunken and in his eyes there was a look of resignation.

"Madame Pothron?" He put a hand on the door jamb as if to steady himself. "I have some news. About your husband, Emile."

CHAPTER 10

I saw them at a hundred yards – the dark green
tanks, rattling slowly and solemnly over the roadway
like a funeral procession, and the black-clad figures
standing in the open turrets with wooden faces ...
- Arthur Koestler

Madame Faure visited Alice the day after her
abortive exodus. She carried the same basket but this
time, instead of eggs, she had a few strawberries
lying like red beating hearts in a nest of green leaves.

"My son told me how you sewed up the wound in
your dog," she said. "You're a brave lady."

"Thank you, Madame," Alice said.

"And the dog?"

"He will live."

"You left, but you came back. Why?"

Alice could not answer. Images of the chaos on
the road were too raw. And then there was the news
about Emile.

"Is something the matter, Madame Pothron?"

Alice could feel her lips trembling. "Yesterday I
had a visit from someone who knows what happened
to my husband. He's in a prisoner-of-war camp. The
man said all prisoners were going to be transported
to Germany."

Madame Faure threw her apron over her head
and keened.

"*Mon Dieu*," she cried. "He'll be placed in one of
their slave labor camps. Be assured, Madame, you'll
never see your husband again."

When Madame Faure left, still moaning and muttering her pessimistic view of Emile's future, Alice picked Evelyne up and ran to her aunt's house. In gasps, she managed to tell Louise what her neighbor had said.

Louise gave her a rough shake. "Really, Alice, you mustn't let yourself go like this," she said. "Of course Emile will come back. Now, stop crying. I always thought you'd go to pieces in a crisis. Anyway, we'll go and speak to Monsieur Jochmans. He'll know what to do. Now, hush, you stupid girl. It's no good sniveling. That's not going to bring Emile home."

The Jochmans were in the kitchen when they arrived; the two older children playing a complicated game with string. The baby, Therese, slept in her mother's arms. Louise explained to the Jochmans about Alice's news and asked what they thought Alice should do. M. Jochmans shook his head sadly and shrugged.

"I think it would be best to wait until you have some official news. Otherwise, it is merely gossip."

Alice thought of Emile who had gone off filled with confidence that the war would soon be over and they would go home to America. Now it was possible they would never see each other again. She felt tears fill her eyes.

Perhaps in order to take Alice's mind away from her bad news the Jochmans questioned her about the exodus; how many people, what about the Luftwaffe, why did she come back? Alice explained as best she could and eventually she dried her eyes, horribly aware there were others whose suffering was greater than hers. At least Emile was alive.

It was after Alice's abortive attempt at escape that M. Jochmans decided the Germans were too close and it was time to take the villagers up to the other farm at Charny. They would stay up in the hills until they deemed it safe to return to Paron. He and other men in the village had already hidden the larger animals. Horses, cattle, a few sheep, all tucked away in the forest where they would be safe from the enemy. Now it was time to save the women and children.

"But school starts in September," Emilienne squealed. "I have to go to school."

"I'm sure we'll be back by then."

"And what about the harvest?" Ferdinand asked.

"We have so much to lose if we leave," Godelieve Jochmans said. "There'll be looters. I've heard the people from the road are breaking into shops in Sens to get food. They'll do the same to our farm, our house."

"I shall come back and stay here. The men in the village are happy to see their wives and children taken to safety but each one has decided to stay and protect their property," M. Jochmans said.

"But what about my Emile?" Alice asked.

Godelieve and Emile Jochmans exchanged glances. Alice read the look and felt cold.

"He will come back, won't he?"

"Yes, yes, of course," Godelieve said. "Come along, everyone, go and pack and we'll leave as soon as possible."

Word passed around Paron and within the hour the women and children had congregated at the Jochmans' farm. The men helped load them onto the various vehicles and slowly the cavalcade moved out of the farmyard. On the back of a truck hens cackled in their makeshift cages, their feathers ruffled by the hot June breeze. Tethered pigs squealed from a hay-stacked trailer. Behind them walked a cow, her udder swinging. The children all crowded onto one cart, chattered and giggled as if on a great adventure.

On the back of the Jochmans' truck Alice clutched Evelyne as they rocked down the road towards Charny. Skippy, not yet well, cowered beside her. They cleared the last house in Paron and their strange little procession moved slowly down the rutted road. Alice kept a wary lookout, remembering her abortive attempt at escape and the diving Stukas.

They joined the ragged refugees still struggling along the road south and drove on the main road to Courtenay. Just beyond was a junction where they turned to Auxerre and then another turn towards La Ferté-Loupièrre. The farm was close by and they would be safe.

But it was not to be.

At the junction of the tree-shaded road to Auxerre they found several Wehrmacht trucks and soldiers lounging in the warm grass.

"Halt," screamed one of them. "Halt."

They stopped and Emile Jochmans got slowly out of the cab and approached an officer. There were hard voices and the men gesticulated and finally shouts filled the air. He came back to the vehicles shaking his head.

"It's hopeless," he said. "We'll have to go back. They won't let us through. We don't have papers, he says."

"What papers?"

M. Jochmans shrugged. "Whatever papers they want, I suppose."

The group turned and headed back to Paron.

It was almost a relief. Alice had tried not once but twice to escape and each time she had been thwarted. It was as if God or fate or nature or whatever had ordained that she, Alice Pothron, would stay in her house in Paron and face whatever was to come. It brought a sense of dull resignation and she hoped that perhaps it was not going to be as bad as people were predicting. The Germans could not be as cruel as folk were saying, could they? They were, after all, people from a refined, educated and advanced society. They had a morality inbred over centuries. They would behave like civilized human beings. Surely they would?

Anyway, to face whatever was coming right here in Paron and in her own home would be better than facing it in a strange place.

It was on her return from this second abortive attempt to escape that Alice found a small yellow postcard waiting for her. It was headed *Kriegsgefangenpost* and it was from Emile. In a few short words he told her of his capture and that he was being held at the Val de Grace Hospital in Paris before being sent to a camp in Germany. It was as Mme Faure had predicted, a camp in Germany with a possibility – no, the probability – that he would never return.

On Saturday 15 June 1940, the Germans arrived in Paron. The town was baking under a heat wave. Right down the street windows and doors stood open as if trying to catch hold of something other than stiflingly hot air. Even the breeze through the windows seemed to come straight off a furnace.

At first, all Alice heard was a slow heavy grinding noise, like far-off thunder, that grew and grew. Then the streets were suddenly filled with German soldiers on motorbikes, in trucks, on tanks. Wave after wave, it seemed, silent and intent.

She held Evelyne tightly in her arms and hid behind the net curtain watching as they drove slowly down the main street of Paron, past Alice's house, past the chapel and on through the rest of the village, spreading out like a grey-green spider's web. Men in uniform, helmets shadowing their eyes, faces stern as they passed, kicking up the dust on their silent way and the dogs ran from them, tails between their legs.

Finally, when they stopped in the street it was almost with a sense of disbelief to see those clean, calm young men standing in the hot June air. They took off their helmets and wiped sweat off their brows, their blond hair blown dry by the soft hot breeze of the summer day. Were these the baby-eating monsters that people feared? They looked so normal, just like the youths of Paron.

She was unprepared for the hammering on her door.

"*Ouvert*. Open at once."

Alice had never believed in the idea of going 'weak at the knees' until this moment. She clung to the back of a kitchen chair, bile thrusting up into her throat, her breath shallow.

The shout came again, louder this time. A fist hammered as if to break down the door. Alice watched in sick terror as the door was shoved open. It slammed against the wall and a tall German officer stalked in, his uniform dusty, his face an arrogant mask.

"Madame, is this your house?" He spoke in schoolbook but perfect French.

"*Oui*," Alice's voice was only a whisper.

"You live here alone?"

"Yes. My child and I."

"Very well." The officer turned and shouted something to the troops outside the door.

"What are you going to do?" Her voice was tremulous.

"You will see," he said.

And Alice did.

The very attributes that Emile had found so attractive about the house; on the main road to Sens, sturdy with a large number of rooms and many windows facing the street, would now serve the Germans well.

Several young soldiers burst into the room. Handsome young men, eyes the deep blue of lakes and hair like early wheat. Each greeted Alice politely as they began setting up their machine guns, tripods first then sandbags to hold them in place. Lastly the guns were unwrapped from cloth, the smell of oil potent. A machine gun was poised on a tripod at each window, pointing out and down the street. Each was manned by two men who, once they'd finished their task, stood to attention as the officer inspected their work and murmured his pleasure at a job well done. With the machine guns in place all exits and entries into Paron were covered.

Within the hour Alice's home had been turned into a German machine gun post with what seemed a dozen or more soldiers milling about waiting for orders.

Her house had been taken over. She had nowhere to go unless Louise was prepared to take her in. Alice went upstairs to pack. Numbly she placed her clothes in an old suitcase. She carefully folded Evelyne's things and placed them on top, then dragged the case down the stairs. The officer stared at her.

"Where are you going?"

"I'll go to relatives. You can have the house."

"Oh no," the officer said smiling. "You will stay here. I need someone to look after my men and you will do very nicely, Madame."

"At least let my child leave and stay with family."

"No."

The officer took Evelyne in his arms. She screamed and reached for her mother. Alice stared at him in horror.

"While the child is here we can count on your co-operation. Don't look so worried, Madame. We will not harm either of you if you do as we say."

He handed Evelyne back.

"By the end of the year we will have crossed the Channel and we'll be in London," he said, a smile on his death's-head face. "Then the war will be over. We can all go home and then once again you may have your house to yourself. In the meantime, it is ours."

Alice went back upstairs and slowly unpacked her case.

CHAPTER 11

Nous sommes en pleine pagaille
We're in a complete mess
- Ian Ousby

The war in France was over in less than seven weeks.

By 18 June 1940, nearly two million French soldiers had been captured, far more than the Germans had expected. Logistical difficulties arose as few preparations had been made for such large numbers. The end result was that prisoners were placed in make-shift camps under conditions of tremendous hardship while awaiting deportation to Germany.

Emile Pothron was among them.

Berlin had sent an administrative force of thirty thousand men and women to Paris where they requisitioned five hundred of the best hotels. They quickly took over the best restaurants, cinemas and brothels for their exclusive use. Soon the ominous black and red swastika flew everywhere as the task of controlling and administering the conquered country began.

It was made easier by their network of spies implanted into French society months, even years, before. As a result, the Germans knew every nook and cranny of the country, the location of every railway station as well as its timetables, every fuel depot, each municipal office, the names of all the officials and public servants. They had long planned the occupation of France, and the change-over from civilian government to military administration went smoothly. The Germans were nothing, if not efficient. The smooth take-over of France was largely the work of the *Militärbefehlshaber* or military Commander-in-Chief, General Otto von Stűlpnagel who was stationed in splendor at the Hotel Majestic on avenue Kléber in Paris. Later in 1942 he was followed by a cousin, Carl-Heinrich von Stűlpnagel. Both men were, first and foremost, military men doing a military job. Neither was a Hitler supporter and held no truck with the Nazis or their instruments of repression and torture. In fact, Carl-Heinrich Stűlpnagel was executed in 1944 as a traitor after the abortive bomb plot against Hitler called Operation Valkyrie.

When Emile and the other men of the Fifth Military Medical Section arrived at the Val de Grace military hospital in Place Alphone-Laveron in the 5th *arrondissement*, they found an ominous ten-foot-high barbed-wire fence running along Boulevard de Port-Royal and a high stone wall in the rear. Guard towers loomed over them from the four corners of the enclosed area and armed sentries stood guard at the gate. The make-shift camp in the hospital grounds was a temporary arrangement until the prisoners could be shipped to Germany.

It proved a recipe for either fatalism or immediate plans for escape.

Not long after their arrival, the *Kommandant* called Captain Delavierre to his office. The prisoners had expertise that could be used in the hospital, he said, and ordered Delavierre to make a list of the men who could work while they were waiting to be taken to a slave labor camp in Germany. By placing Captain

Delavierre in a position of trust and authority the German *Kommandant* ensured the good behavior of the prisoners. They could also inflict their type of discipline, but at one remove from their captives.

Emile's first task was to assist with the x-rays of two Wehrmacht soldiers who had been injured in a traffic accident. He did as he was ordered, then helped push the gurneys from the x-ray department back to the ward. He noticed the wards were strictly allocated; the best, of course, for German officers.

On another floor he observed a prison ward for captured Allied soldiers and airmen and a different one for civilians. This civilian ward puzzled Emile until Delavierre offered a possible explanation. The Germans had plans to invade England in September, he said. It meant the enemy needed complete control of towns like Dunkirk, Calais and Dieppe in order to facilitate the assault. The residents of this area were probably unable to return to their homes and, he had heard, were being kept in camps in Paris. Delavierre later confirmed this to be the case after speaking to some of the civilian patients.

Emile made a mental note of the information – who knew when it would come in handy?

As one of the senior officers at the camp, Captain Delavierre set about creating a sense of order. He recognized it would be important for the men to keep their minds focused on the job at hand, that is, survival as a prisoner-of-war, and stop them talking about a doubtful future in a slave labor camp in Germany. He realized the men's attitudes would be important if they were to survive. As it was, uncertainty rode like vultures on their shoulders. Corrosive rumors roiled around the camp, feeding on fear and despair. There were stories promising early release or imminent departure by train for Germany and stories of massacres and reprisals. As a result, the prisoners lived at the extreme edge of fear rendering them more fearful, more hopeless and therefore more vulnerable.

Early morning *appel* or roll call in the *appelplatz* was the worst time. The anticipated news of a train journey to Germany would probably be announced at *appel,* so the men stood almost paralyzed with fear until the counting was over and they could return to their duties.

Keep your head down, better to be safe, Delavierre told his men, we'll be released soon. But not all agreed. In desperation, some tried escaping over the stone wall at the rear of the camp. They were never heard of again. No one knew if they had successfully escaped or if they had been captured and shot. Such uncertainty was more debilitating than the misery, hunger or the claustrophobic life they led in Val de Grace.

Once the Armistice was signed, and the prisoners learned of this very early on, they expected to be returned home. There was a clause in the Armistice document that French prisoners would be released once hostilities ended. Few realized that meant with the defeat of Britain. They conjectured it would only be a matter of weeks before they went home. But their hopes were dashed as the days, weeks and then months went slowly by and England hung on and then began to fight back. Delavierre agreed with Emile that a person convicted of a crime knew the length of his sentence. As prisoners-of-war they did not know and that was what ate into them, not knowing how long it would be before they were free.

As the months passed the symptoms of malnutrition; weight loss, a certain mental confusion and irritability, began to manifest. Men fought over trivia or they cried in corners not remembering afterwards what their tears were for. Emile wondered if he would die right here in this awful place and never see his beloved Alice or his child again.

As an officer, Captain Delavierre had been asked, and had given his word, that he would not attempt to escape. It had its advantages. He was allowed to drive an ambulance out of the camp and into Paris to pick up patients. As he studied the routines of the guards and the route into Paris, he wondered how he could put this new freedom to good use. Early on he had made the brave decision to help his men escape the prison camp before they were sent to Germany and almost certain death. All Captain Delavierre needed was one trusted friend on the outside. He found him, stomping along the street, with a folded newspaper in his pocket.

Delavierre stopped the ambulance and called out. The man looked up.

"*Docteur* Delavierre? *Mon Dieu.*"

They sat in a small bistro with the ambulance parked nearby, each with a cup of the *café national* a bitter acorn brew that passed for coffee. Delavierre examined the wizened brown face.

"I'm glad you remember me," he said. "Verdun. Left leg, off below the knee. I'm afraid your name escapes me."

"No names, *Docteur*. Better that way."

They began tentatively circling around; probing each other's opinions, discussing the woeful state of affairs into which France had fallen. Both agreed that, in spite of the initial show of good manners, the Germans would soon set about a campaign of humiliation, intimidation, imprisonment and death.

"We keep our heads down and our own counsel. It's difficult. No one knows who is friend or who is foe," the man said.

Delavierre agreed; not every Frenchman could be trusted.

"Resistance?"

The man shrugged. "There is none. Not that I've noticed. A little graffiti here and there, a boy shot for cutting telephone wires and people are forbidden to wear the Tricolor on their jackets. Some do, some don't. But generally people are waiting to see."

"And what about collaboration?"

"Widespread, I'm afraid. France is anticipating a long occupation. People feel they have to live and if collaboration is the price, then that's what they'll do. Hitler has promised a thousand-year Reich, so people are settling in for the long haul."

"And you?"

The one-legged man scowled. "Never," he said, thumping the table with his fist.

Delavierre had found his man.

After that initial meeting, they sat from time to time in the small bistro and drank *ersatz* coffee, the ambulance nearby. Eventually Delavierre explained his plan, his need of one person from whom an escape line could develop. The man nodded his understanding and they parted on a handshake.

It took time and Delavierre wisely asked no questions. But finally there was someone who was ready to house an escapee, one who knew someone to supply clothes and another who worked at the *Kommandantur* on Place de l'Opera who could lay her hands on the requisite stamps. Delavierre assumed they also had a photographer and a good forger who could make copies of the permits required for travel and identification. It took months but by the end of

1940 it was ready. All they needed was one brave young man to test it.

Delavierre wondered who among his men would be the first. But it really did not take much thought.

Emile Pothron, *l'Américain.*

Emile was sharp, calculating and determined. He was also a survivor. He had all the signs of a street fighter, but with a gentle side to his nature. Delavierre liked that in the boy and imagined little Alice Pothron, of whom he had heard so much, had something to do with it. If anyone could survive on the run it would be Emile Pothron.

Yes, young Pothron was the man, Delavierre thought.

Good.

CHAPTER 12

For a time, in the autumn of 1940,
French experts feared famine ...
- Richard Vinen

If the occupation of her home by a large number of enemy soldiers was not enough, in September 1940 Alice had another stark reminder of war. Food was to be rationed.

She went to the local *hôtel de ville* – the town hall – with her *carte d'identité,* stood in line with every resident of the area in order to receive her ration book and one for Evelyne. Then she registered with the local grocery supplier as well as the *boucherie* – the butcher – and the *boulangerie* – the baker. In future, whenever she bought anything she would have to produce her French identity card and the tiny ration book consisting of small stamps. Each stamp would then be cut out by the relevant supplier.

It was supposed to ensure that everyone had enough to eat, to control prices, to stop inflation and panic, and to prevent hoarding. It did no such thing.

On the day she received her ration card, Alice checked what she could buy and was appalled by the paucity of food allowed. Children under six years-old would get one and a half pints of milk a day. At least Evelyne would be alright. But adults were not nearly so fortunate.

Alice was allowed twelve ounces of bread a day or three hundred and fifty grams. Not much, only a slice or two of the heavy black bread available, but perhaps enough if there were other things. But everything was about to be rationed and Alice soon realized they were in for a very hard time indeed. Ten and a half ounces of meat per week – three hundred grams. *Mon Dieu!* How would she survive? Not quite two ounces of cheese – fifty grams – and seventeen and a half ounces of sugar per month – five hundred grams. A month!

Alice could not believe what she was reading.

Butter was also severely rationed, only seven ounces per month or two hundred grams every thirty days. She could redeem her butter coupons on only one day a month when *l'épicière* received her supplies. Eventually, a kilo of butter would cost a thousand francs. But for the present, prices looked manageable, just, even if there was little to buy.

Finding enough food for the family, heating and, to a lesser degree, clothing now became major concerns. Alice heard that starvation was already an issue in cities like Paris. It seemed inconceivable there could be famine in such a fertile country. To make matters worse, it was rumored that the Germans were taking nearly eighty percent of all produce either for *l'Occupant* – the occupying forces – or to send back to Germany.

In addition to rationing, the Germans had allowed both the franc and the *Reichsmark* as legal currency. But one *Reichsmark* was worth twenty francs so it was just another way of impoverishing the country and further exacerbating the food shortages.

In rural areas such as Paron, they fared a little better as they were close to the source of production of a number of food items. They also had the space to grow at least some vegetables and fruit and have a few rabbits or chickens in the garden. Instead, rural people found themselves deprived of clothing, fertilizer, soap and luxuries such as coffee, tea and sugar. Fuel was also a big issue. With coal no longer available, wood had to be gathered wherever it could be found. Alice got into the habit of foraging along the railroad as friendly train drivers would often throw coal off the steam locomotives to waiting villagers. It was black gold.

Alice soon learned the unfamiliar tasks of hoeing and planting and of caring for small livestock. In summer her garden flourished, the rabbits procreated and the hens provided a few eggs. M. Jochmans continued to be a generous and necessary butcher as Alice never got used to that nauseating task.

Private barter systems sprang up between families, friends and acquaintances. City dwellers connected to someone, anyone, in the country made full use of the relationship. Bartering between townies and their country cousins became the norm; food for blouses, shoes or overcoats. In an area like Paron, locally grown wines became valuable tools for barter and a few canny villagers made money selling home brewed wine in the cities. Cigarettes were popular bargaining items, but there was a problem. Women were legally banned from obtaining cigarettes on their ration cards so this method of barter was closed to Alice.

Although she never starved, food was always on her mind. Alice dreamed up menus as she carried water from the pump or washed the soldier's clothes in the wash house. She remembered the vast buffet on the *Normandie,* and restaurants in New York, Boston and San Francisco where she and Emile had dined. Alice wondered if she would ever eat like that again. She longed for a plate of clam chowder served with sourdough bread or a Thanksgiving turkey followed by pumpkin pie. She had never appreciated food so much as when she had so little.

Shopping for food became a major occupation. Women began lining up outside the stores from very early in the morning, often before dawn. Some people made a 'career' out of lining up for others and charged seven francs an hour for their time. Most stood patiently in snow or wind or, when summer came, in the heat. Those who, like Alice, cooked for German 'guests' were given special rights to go to the head of the food lines. But she could not face the antagonism of other shoppers so she took her place in the line, determined not to be singled out. She already suffered from the muttered charge of 'horizontal collaboration' because she had Germans in her house. She could not bear to have more anger directed at her and Evelyne.

Like most people, Alice had to balance her life between accommodating the soldiers and retaining her dignity in the face of the invaders. She was not the only one to have German soldiers billeted in her house, not the only woman who was shopping for *l'Occupant*. Louise and Jules were in the same position and there were others. She had hoped most villagers would understand that this was not of her choosing. But, once again, being a 'foreigner' played against her as many villagers thought she was rather strange and therefore capable of anything.

Even she had to admit it; she was different. Alice had not lived an adult life in main-stream France. It was obvious and easily gave rise to the accusation of 'strangeness'. Her childhood and teenage years had been lived within the walls of the orphanage and so she had little concept of what life was like in an ordinary French home. Her adult experience had been in America where things were radically different. She was used to electricity and easy phone calls, food available at the local Piggly Wiggly supermarket. She wore clothes that were markedly different from the long rusty-black garments of her neighbors. Her dresses were in vivid colors with skirts considerably shorter than was the norm in a rural village. That was not how rural French women dressed.

Even her accent was different. It had mellowed and rounded after ten years in America. In order to allay suspicion, she had told the inquisitive she was from Paris where, according to gossip, just about anything was tolerated. Most seemed to accept her story and regarded her slightly accented French - and her inability to make *boeuf bourguignon* from the red wine and Charollais beef of the area - as proof of city-life decadence. Several muttered that she must have had servants as she seemed particularly inept – according to Paron standards – in both home and garden. She struggled with the stove and the water pump and planted flowers instead of vegetables. It was rumored she even had to get the neighbor to wring the necks of her chickens. *Mon Dieu, quel prochain?* What next, indeed.

To some extent, the generosity and friendship of the Jochmans protected Alice and Evelyne. The locals respected Godelieve and Emile, who were straight and honest in their dealings with the villagers. The general consensus was, if the Jochmans approved of the strange little Parisian, then she was probably alright. But it was said with some hesitation and a warning that no good would come of her acquaintance with the local prostitute.

Once food shortages began to impact, the French people, ever resilient and innovative, started to improvise. They ate turnips which, before the invasion, were considered stock feed. They toasted ground acorns and barley mixed with chicory and made a bitter and barely palatable substitute for imported coffee. Called *café national* it was served with a grapo sweetener that did little to improve the taste. The French went without sugar, rice, tea, baked goods and meat. In cities and large towns, residents ate guinea pigs, pigeons caught in the parks and cats – although the authorities were quick to caution that eating cats was unhealthy. Alice kept a close eye on Skippy, lest someone steal him for the pot.

The Germans in her house brought in requisitioned or stolen food. They made sure they never went without. She sometimes shared their largesse, after all, she had to cook it, and she had no compunction about feeding Evelyne out of the soldiers' rations.

Alice generally kept to herself, never knowing who of her neighbors to trust or who was collaborating. Unless they knew each other intimately, neighbors tended to keep away from each other in case they were denounced for reckless talk. Denouncement meant arrest, arrest meant interrogation, interrogation meant torture and, as the weeks turned into months of savage occupation, everyone seemed to know of someone who had been arrested. Sometimes those who had been denounced did not come home. Denouncement often came from collaborators protecting their patch and people knew who they were; they were the ones who could still eat meat and drink real coffee. People crossed the street rather than have to greet a known collaborator. They would keep their revenge sweet until after the war.

The red flag with the black crawling spider was everywhere. Germans soldiers were everywhere, demanding food or wine, often at gunpoint. Punishment for any perceived or real resistance was immediate and often fatal. The people of Paron, of France, never knew when to expect a visit from the *gendarmerie* or the Gestapo.

And death by bullet or torture could come at any time.

CHAPTER 13

Women's traditional ability to
improvise and adapt served them well
during the German occupation
- Margaret Collins Weitz

Winter 1940/41. The soldiers had been in her house for six months and there seemed to be no end to their unwelcome presence.

It was as desperately cold as the previous winter had been, perhaps worse. Snow flurried in at the beginning of November and the roof tops glittered under a mantle of white. It gathered on scarves and sat on shoulders like white epaulettes.

Alice remembered the previous winter when she and Evelyne had slept in the kitchen, cozy and snug before the stove. This time it was the soldiers who enjoyed the kitchen's warmth while Alice and Evelyne shivered upstairs. She said a private prayer of gratitude that she did not have to sleep in the cellar.

By December they had run out of requisitioned coal and only the officers in the Chateau across the road were warm that Christmas. Alice could see the smoke drifting from the Chateau's chimneys, imagined the officers, their leather-encased legs close to the roaring fire and Hitler's face staring from a portrait above the mantelpiece. The officers did very well indeed, living in comparative luxury in the commandeered Chateau while the ordinary soldiers in Alice's house were not much better off than she was.

The Chateau - 2010

They crowded into the kitchen, the only warm room of the house, smoking, chattering, playing cards and passing around photographs of girlfriends, fat smiling *fraulein* with blonde plaits garlanding their heads. Take away their rigid field-grey uniforms and they were really very ordinary young men who would rather have been home with their *junge damen* and their beer and sausage and *spaetzle,* the fatty noodles of which they spoke with such nostalgia.

Each morning they clattered out to drill, always leaving behind a small crew to man the machine guns so she was never free of them. Initially, they were polite and treated Alice with a level of respect, carried in wood and sometimes even a bucket of water from the pump. Some of the officers frequented the Jochmans' farm where their horses were stabled, watching the grooming and the prancing of their favorites. M. Jochmans told Alice that an officer was teaching Emilienne to ride. They weren't all bad, he said ruefully. But still Alice feared these men with a dark foreboding.

She was getting used to the ritual of lining up for rationed food. The two-mile walk to Sens early in the morning, with an oft-times crabby Evelyne, was now a habit. She stood in line with the other women, silhouettes in the dark. She greeted the women whose faces she was now beginning to recognize.

"Bonjour, Madame. Bonjour. Il fait très froid ce matin?"

No one wanted to discuss how they were. It was obvious; they were cold, hungry and defeated. There were few blue-lipped smiles on those icy mornings. By summer the women were too tired, too thin to care much about the niceties of good behavior.

The lines of women formed in front of the *boulangerie* and the *boucherie* where a scrag-end of bone would make a pot of soup for a family. There was always a column snaking along the sidewalk with women yawning, scratching, murmuring and stamping their numb feet. String bags held in work-worn hands, they were ready to buy whatever was available.

To pass the time they sometimes conjured up meals they had enjoyed before the 'damned Fritzes' arrived.

"... a plate of *bouillabaisse*," one woman said. "My mother-in-law is from Marseille, bless her. She taught me how to make the real thing. Oysters, shrimps, crab ..."

"... and some garlic ..."

"... and tomato. Must be rich and red."

Alice did not divulge that she would give anything for a real New York hot dog with ketchup and onions. She could almost taste the sheer luxury of a well presented hot dog on a white crusty bread roll. Or a bowl of clam chowder she and Emile had enjoyed at their favorite Monterey restaurant in California. Now, that was worth a dream or two. Or perhaps cracking open a lobster at Bar Harbor, bibs tucked around their necks and butter dripping off their chins.

In the aching pre-dawn chill two ill-clad women behind Alice breathed out tobacco smoke and gossip into the air. These are all such brave women. The world is ending all around them and still they endure, Alice thought admiringly. They survive because they are needed, by their children, by their husbands, by their country. But it was hard, so hard.

In that December, even the heavens seemed determined to increase their misery. The early morning snow had been tramped to sludge that crept into broken shoes. Tendrils of cold mist hung like muslin from the skeleton arms of trees. Cloud hung low, folding down on them from the hills around Paron. It was going to be another icy day.

"Have you heard about Vichy's new scheme?"

"Which one's that?"

"They're going to pay us to have babies."

"No!"

"Yes, it's true. They're going to pay us to have babies so we can increase the population."

"Where are we going to find a man? You tell me that!"

An old crone cackled. "I'm going to have to find a nice young boyfriend."

"You silly old hag. You think you're *une bombe*? Hey? A hot one? Any man would need to be blind and drunk to go with you!"

It was good to laugh, even at that early hour when a chill wind moaned around corners, dragging at coats and sneaking through thin blouses. Alice's reward for the two-hour wait that day was a loaf of stale bread and a few parsnips. Her winter garden yielded some parsley and that was about all. Supper would be boiled parsnips with a smattering of parsley. It could be worse, she thought.

Alice's first task each morning, long before the sun rose into a violet sky, was to clean out yesterday's ashes from stove and set the fire going. The soldiers had not yet stirred as she arranged some sticks and newspaper. Soon the warmth dissolved the harsh air and set the window panes dripping. As the kettle started to sing the men awoke. Their straw pallets rustled as they stood up and stretched. She left them to dress while she took Evelyne outside.

Her next task was to bring in enough water for the day. The iron handle of the bucket was sometimes so cold her fingers stuck to the metal. The Germans had found a second bucket and she would return to the kitchen twice-burdened, her cold feet crunching on the new-laid snow. Sometimes, on the gruff-voiced command of one of the soldiers, she would go back to the pump.

Over the months the pump became a symbol of her slavery. She wondered how many times she had drawn water from the mouth of that iron monster. It seemed an eternity that she stood, sometimes counting the number of times she depressed the handle, but mostly she just pumped in a daze, getting it over with.

The pump at Alice's house

In the summer mornings the soldiers crowded round the water pump, shirts hanging from their trousers as they washed their sleep-reddened faces and bodies. The pump and its life-giving water was the one common factor that bound them together. And she hated it.

Stove cleaned and fueled and a bucket or two of water in for the morning. Then it was time to fix breakfast. As she cut the black loaf of bread into equal slices, the corporal, the one with hair the color of old washing and a mouth wide-lipped and wet, leaned over her. He was a little older than the rest, his frame angular with muscles that looked as if they were held together with baling wire. He smiled at her, more than a smile, it was a *'guten morgen'* wrapped in a smirk. She felt his eyes like snails over her flesh.

"I like French women," he once said. "They are so ... generous."

Fear remained a constant, fear of that corporal, fear of the men and what they were capable of. It crystallized early one morning when she left Evelyne in the warm kitchen and went to the outhouse at the back of the garden. The soldiers were still asleep, boots in neat rows at the end of their straw pallets, their breath expelling noisily into the dawn. When she returned she found Evelyne playing a jumping game over the soldiers' boots.

She swept the child away in a surge of horror.

"No, Evelyne. Not near them. Never, you understand."

She gave Evelyne a little shake and when the child began to cry held her close with murmurs of solace on her lips.

Mondays were washdays; the day she hated most. On Sunday nights her last duty was to carry loads of dirty clothing out into the backyard where, in winter, frost creaked like old leather under her feet and the smell of sour sweat and stale cigarettes seemed to linger on her fingers. She placed everything in an old tin tub for soaking. It took many buckets of water to fill, back-breaking trips to the water pump. In the morning she wrung the clothes out and took them to the wash house behind the church.

Soap was in short supply. Advice in the newspaper was to soak clothes overnight in a solution of wood ash and then rub the clothes on stones. She tried rubbing the clothing on the stone edge of the wash trough but it never seemed to work. Everything was beginning to look grey and frayed.

The first winter of the occupation seemed to last forever. No matter how well she wrapped up, Alice was always cold. Chilblains and blisters from the pump handle brought her untold misery. Breaking the ice from the wash trough was pure agony. It reminded her of earlier days that she had tried to forget. It was like being back in the orphanage. Once again she was washing someone else's clothes, her fingers red with cold while plunging the dirty stinking garments into chilled and slow-moving water.

Afterwards she dragged a tub full of wet clothes across the road and home to hang in the back yard on the rope washing line; very often with Evelyne stumbling behind her, thumb in mouth and eyelids puffy from lack of sleep.

One Monday morning, when a weak sun was making an effort to break through the veil of mist, the local priest stuck his head around the wash house door and greeted her with a small blessing. She wondered if he watched out for her, because there were many occasions when he suddenly appeared just as it was time to heave the heavy tub of wet washing back to the house. He would smile as he took one side and together they walked it across the road and into her backyard.

The wash house

This time there was a mischievous grin on his hollow face. Without a word he slipped a bar of soap into her hand, put a finger to his lips then walked across the road and into the small stone chapel.

Real soap, the first she had seen in months. She slipped it into her pocket, a small blessing in a harsh world.

In January 1941, the town was still endlessly white. February then March and winter clung on like a bad deed. The snow turned to black ice and then to dark dirty sludgy water that lay in the gutters. By late March the men were still sleeping as close to the stove as they could get. At the beginning of April it had finally begun to warm and blossoms appeared on the apple trees, shyly hanging in clusters from overloaded branches. Only then did the soldiers move out of the kitchen and into their designated rooms. The kitchen was finally free of them and Alice could open the windows and get rid of the stink of too many human bodies clustered too close together.

The officer in charge lived in the Chateau and often visited his billeted men and ordered new tasks. The young soldiers stripped down the machine guns, oiled them and re-assembled the parts. Now that it was summer and the heat began early, he took them on dawn route marches and brought them back dripping with sweat. He was a middle-aged man, this officer, handsome in a bland sort of way; his blond hair parted in the middle and slicked down with perfumed oil. Alice thought he had stepped out of a Rembrandt painting, with his too-clever eyes and a sensuous mouth pursed in a feminine pout.

She could barely endure his presence, his eloquence and his gentlemanly manners. He was the one who had come into her house that first morning, who had ordered the setting up of the machine gun posts at her windows. He was the one who had imprisoned her and forced her to be a slave for these odious young men; and so she hated him, hated his sleek looks and his long thin fingers that rapped endlessly on the table. He epitomized the enemy who, she had found, had only a thin veneer of civil decency covering the beast within.

This predator with his clean hair and good clothing sat at her kitchen table and enjoyed her misery. He was a young man who barely saw her humanity and treated her with condescension, as if she were invisible.

There was surely nothing more they could do that they had not already done. Nothing could be as bad as being a servant to these odious young men. But she was wrong.

CHAPTER 14

No praise is too high for the courage of the
anonymous people of France. They sought no
rewards, no honours. They gave their homes and
their lives because, in their simple code of honour,
their country demanded them.
- Maurice Buckmaster

Val de Grace prison camp, 1940. Emile felt that winter had arrived early and with menace. The morning sunlight was sharp but its warmth barely penetrated the men standing to attention in the *appelplatz*. The wind was freezing and thin men shivered in their inadequate clothing. All were suffering some degree of hunger and were twitchy and stressed with the circumstances as well as the unknown and forbidding future. They stood on the parade ground stamping their feet and blowing on blue fingers.

The seventy men of the Fifth Military Medical Section – five of the original number had made an escape attempt and no one knew whether they had made it or not – had been in the prisoner-of-war camp for almost six months with the dread of imminent mass deportation hanging over their heads. None knew the time or day and, although they knew as little as the prisoners, the guards continually reminded them that their time was short.

As they dispersed after roll-call Captain Delavierre beckoned Emile over. They walked slowly into the lee of a building where they would be out of the cold wind.

"Transportation to Germany is definitely on the cards," Delavierre said. "The *Kommandant* warned me to prepare the men for evacuation."

"That doesn't mean anything. He could be toying with us."

Emile and the other men had fallen for that trick too many times for him to be worried. But he had to admit the guards had seemed more edgy, more ready to shoot. They had begun to check the numbers more often and more men seemed to land up in the punishment block. They sensed something was about to happen.

"Are they really here for a thousand years?" Emile asked Delavierre. "What do you think?"

Delavierre shrugged as they began to walk the periphery of the camp. From the wooden towers above armed German guards eyed them warily.

"I notice you're keeping yourself fit," Delavierre said.

"Nothing else to do, is there?"

"Press-ups and jogging while the rest of the men just lie around? I'm impressed."

Emile did not want to tell Delavierre his exercise regime was getting harder to do. He could feel himself slowly getting weaker. Deportation to Germany loomed large in his thoughts, as it did for all the men. He wondered if, in his present condition, he would make it if they were marched out and put into cattle trucks for a long train trip to Germany.

Delavierre stopped and quite suddenly said, "Would you like to see San Francisco again?"

The question caught Emile off-guard. He felt tears burn his eyes.

"I would do anything if it were possible," he whispered.

"Well, we'll see," Delavierre said, patting Emile on the shoulder. "You're on shift in a half-hour. Now, get to work. We'll talk again soon."

Delavierre approached him again in the middle of November. "I think it's time for you to get out of here, *mon ami.*"

"A dream," Emile said. "I can't afford dreams anymore."

"You want to get back to America? You can't do that by sitting on your skinny little *derrière* here in the camp. I can help you if you want to get out."

"Of course I want to get out. But how?"

"Leave it to me," Delavierre said.

Emile was suddenly determined.

"If I got out the first thing I would do is go to Paron, to get Alice and then to the American Embassy. Mr. Bullitt may still be there."

But Delavierre shook his head. "The Embassy is closed and going to Paron is dangerous. Your best bet would be to go south, to the unoccupied zone. You might find a few American consulate offices still operating there."

It was Thursday 28 November 1940, just after roll-call when Delavierre beckoned to Emile. It was time. He went to his bunk, stuffed his few belongings into his pockets and joined the Captain at the ambulance. They got into the cab and Emile drove carefully towards the gate. As usual, there was a guard standing just inside, stamping his feet and smoking.

"Let me do the talking," Delavierre said. "I know this guy. He's bone lazy and can be bought for a cigarette."

Emile stopped just short of the gate. His fingers tapped a nervous staccato on the steering wheel. The guard sauntered up to Delavierre, his rifle hanging casually from a shoulder.

"Guten morgen, Herr Doktor."

The guard casually checked Delavierre's authorization. Emile held his breath.

"Gut," the guard said, taking the offered cigarette from Delavierre and waving him on. *"Raus!"* Get out. Go.

Emile drove carefully out of the gates of Val de Grace and into the chill morning air of Paris. Was it that easy, he wondered?

Other thoughts clamored in his brain. What now? What had Delavierre planned? Would his Captain be safe going back? What if someone noticed there was only one man in the ambulance instead of the two that had gone out? Then Emile realized the ingenuity of the plan. Two men had indeed gone out of the gate. Delavierre was going to pick up a patient – so two men would be returning. Simple, especially if the person Delavierre picked up sat in the front as sometimes happened.

"I'll drop you off in the city," said Delavierre. "You'll be met by a friend."

"Are you going to be safe when you return? Will the trick work?"

Delavierre smiled. "I've been watching them. I'll go back after the guard change. If this works, I hope I can get more of the guys out."

"And what about you, sir? If they discover what you're doing they'll shoot you."

Delavierre shrugged. *"C'est la vie.* I gave my word as a Frenchman and an officer that I wouldn't escape. And, of course, I won't. That's why they give me the freedom to come and go."

"But you didn't give your word that you wouldn't help others to escape."

"That is so," Delavierre grinned suddenly, the look of a naughty schoolboy on his grizzled face. "I made no promises in that regard, so I break no promises."

"And this man I am to meet?"

"Trust me, Emile. He's one of the good guys."

As they drove through Paris, Emile could not help noticing a very different city from the one he had shown Alice not so long ago. The streets were as crowded as they had been in 1938, but a general air of lassitude showed in the dejected slope of shoulders. In 1938, there had been an air of gaiety, almost frivolity. It was nowhere this November 1940. Instead, it was a scene of loss, humiliation and despair.

As Emile steered the ambulance down narrow streets, Delavierre explained how his regular trips out of the Val de Grace prison camp had given him the idea of helping his men escape. He had made a study of the changes of guard, made friends with the laziest, knew their habits and something about their lives back home. He had thereby won their confidence.

He also knew if he drove out with an assistant, by the time the guards changed he could safely drive in without one. He admitted he had not done it before and Emile was a guinea pig. The only problem would be morning roll call. He was relying on the acceptance by the guards of a wrong head-count, which happened from time to time, as some of the men would be on duty in the hospital and not available for counting.

Delavierre explained he knew and trusted the man who would receive the 'parcel' from the ambulance, but after that he remained deliberately ignorant in case he was discovered aiding an escapee. He did not want to be in a position of giving away information under torture. Better not to know, he explained.

In a narrow street not far from *Gare Montparnasse,* Emile pulled over and the two men sat silently as the engine cooled. The city around them was busy with commuters hurrying to the Metro. It seemed to Emile they were doing so without making a sound. It was like a silent movie, all bustle and no noise. Nerves crackled under his skin.

"Cross *Boulevard Pasteur* and go down *rue du Contentin.* On the corner of *Falguiere* you'll see a man with a wooden leg. He will be reading a newspaper. He's waiting for you."

"Thank you," Emile said gruffly.

"*Bonne chance* and go safely back to your America."

Emile clasped Delavierre's hand in both of his.

"*Au revoir, mon Capitaine.*"

With a stab of grief Emile realized he would probably never see his Captain again. He slipped out of the ambulance and stood on the cold sidewalk watching as Delavierre accelerated away.

He found the one-legged man as Delavierre had said, leaning against a building reading the daily newspaper, the *Paris-Soir.* As Emile approached he folded the newspaper and shoved it into his pocket.

"Rabid German rubbish," he grumbled, as he stomped away. "Newspapers all kowtowing to the bastards."

Emile followed, the two men walking quickly over the cobbled sidewalk. At the corner they turned and then again until Emile felt bewildered and totally lost. In a narrow street the man stopped, jerked his thumb at a heavy carriage door.

"Au revoir, monsieur. Bonne chance." He limped away, grumbling under his breath, the offending newspaper still in his pocket.

The double carriage door squeaked as Emile pushed it open. He walked down a short dark passage and then a bright sunlit courtyard opened out before him. A man stood at one of the doors, smoking a cigarette. He nipped off the glowing end of the cigarette, dropped it to the ground and stuffed the rest into his pocket. Then he beckoned and walked inside.

Emile followed him, down a narrow flight of stairs and into a cavernous cellar where pink limestone arches glittered in the lamplight. The man gestured to a chair on which lay a shirt and tie. Emile changed and sat down, a professional looking camera pointed his way. A flash or two and the camera and photographer disappeared up the stairs. No one spoke as Emile put his old uniform back on, just a quick smile from one of the silent men.

At a table a carafe of wine, some black bread and cheese and a small bunch of Muscat grapes were set before him. He was ravenous and tore at the bread and cheese with his teeth, gulped down the red wine and then wolfed down the grapes, until all that was left were bare stalks. It was the first nearly decent meal he'd had in months. Later, he fell asleep on a rough bed with a mattress of straw and a thin grey blanket.

Never had a bed seemed so comfortable or so welcome.

He stayed in the cellar for a few days. Two or three? He lost count. They fed him and let him sleep.

Then another man brought him a set of laborer's clothes, a rough shirt, the ubiquitous French beret, overalls and sturdy boots. Also a warm *Canadienne*, a waterproof jacket lined with lamb's wool. In addition, he was handed a fistful of documents.

"You don't know where you are and you don't know who helped you. Is that understood?"

"Completely."

According to the documents, his name was now Yves Dumont and that he had been born in Paris. The occupation was that of the real Emile Pothron – mechanic. He would have to learn his new identity by heart so that if he were woken in the middle of the night he could recite the details. His memory of the two years he had spent as a child on the streets of Paris would come in handy.

The man advised him to go to *Gare d'Austerlitz* and take the train south. He was handed the requisite travel authorization, a *sauf-conduit* as well as a *carte de travail*, a workman's card.

"Your story is you are going to Montluçon to work. You will meet up with someone there who will get you through the demarcation line just north of the town. This travel document won't take you right through on the train. We don't have one of those for you."

"Right through to where?" Emile asked.

The man looked surprised. "To Spain, of course."

Emile explained he had one important task to do before leaving. He had to go to Paron and see his wife and child, perhaps even persuade her to leave with him. His ache for her was physical, a rough torment somewhere in his gut. There had been no letters in recent weeks. He did not like to think why and hoped they were only being held up by the censors. He wondered how she was managing. She had been so fragile when he left her. The birth of Evelyne had taken its toll and he wondered if she had regained her strength and if she would be well enough to leave Paron on the risky escape route planned for him. And what about the baby? He knew nothing about babies. Was she walking? Talking? Could they escape with a baby?

Whatever the outcome, he had to see her.

It was his love for Alice that had given him the strength to survive the months in Val de Grace. He had seen other men who had no ambition and no plans for life after the war. They were the ones who turned their faces to the wall and would eventually die. He had taken on Delavierre's belief that the ones with purpose and with someone or something to live for were the ones who would survive. He, Emile, had Alice and Evelyne to live for. He had America to live for. He was going to get his family back to San Francisco and no damned German was going to stand in his way.

Early in the morning he took the Metro to Bercy and from there the train for Sens, sixty-two miles away. On the station platform he was pleased to see the throng of impatient men and women pushing through the barriers. A *gendarme* tried to control the crowd, whistling and gesticulating, but was not being terribly successful. It meant there would be only a cursory examination of documents and his forged ones would pass muster. When the train arrived, the waiting crowd surged forward taking Emile with them. There was no room to sit and he stood in the corridor rather than endure the yawning workers and their smell of garlic and sweat.

The river of men and women changed at each station, flowing in and out of the carriages, faces varying – young, old, sick, tired – but all with dull acceptance etched in wrinkles and down-turned mouths. Soon he found a place to sit in the third-class carriage, the wooden seat hard on his thin body. Villages flashed past, too fast for him to see the names. He fought sleep, afraid of the possibility of capture, afraid he would be swept past Sens.

The train slowed and then ground to a stop. The conductor walked up and down the carriages and in a loud voice explained that the line was damaged and they would have to walk part of the way. There was a general mumble of grievance, but the passengers jumped to the ground and began a slow walk along the side of the railway line and around a group of laborers toiling in the weak sunlight. A few miles down the line another train awaited them. They all piled in and continued their journey.

Had someone wrecked the line? Was it deliberate or just the result of poor or inadequate maintenance? Emile liked to think that perhaps the French were finally fighting back.

Later in the morning, he left the train just before it entered Sens, jumping from the carriage as the locomotive slowed and marching briskly as if on an important errand.

A heavy fall of snow muffled the ordinary sounds of the town; the clanking of milk churns, the anxious crowing of a bedraggled and tardy rooster, folk hurrying through the snow. A church bell rang as if under water. His own footsteps crunched on the gravel between the train tracks. Then he was off the tracks and along the river bank. Underfoot a grey slippery mush of old leaves made walking treacherous.

He stopped for a meal at a small bistro; soup, bread, a cup of coffee and a small cognac to keep the cold at bay, all the while watching the river traffic. He noted the number of small heavily-laden craft, grey-uniformed Germans at the helm, coming from the north. A discarded newspaper did little to update him; he did not know whether it was false propaganda he was reading or the truth. He decided it was probably lies. If all these German victories were true, then why was the war still going on?

He whiled away as much time as he could in the bistro re-reading the headlines until he knew them by heart, fearful that someone would note his presence and become curious. Then when he was getting a little desperate the bistro owner caught his eye, gesticulated with his head and Emile followed him into the back. The owner pointed to a small heap of potatoes. "Make yourself useful," he said, and Emile gratefully sat down and peeled potatoes and parsnips until late afternoon. For his trouble the bistro owner gave him a free meal of fish and a few of the potatoes he had peeled and Emile left just as the sun was settling onto the horizon.

The Yonne River was harder to cross. A guard post and a striped rail across the entrance to the bridge indicated the Germans were keeping an eye on things. Emile waited until a lumbering cart filled with hay passed slowly by, the rake-thin horse heaving and snorting. He grabbed hold of the side and hoisted himself up and fell into the hay. A German guard spoke briefly to the farmer, lifted the rail and the old spavined horse shambled over the bridge and into the trees on the other side where Emile jumped free.

He waited until dark before venturing further. Finally he stood in the lee of the small church opposite his house, so close to Alice he could almost feel her. The light faded and it grew colder. Emile stamped his feet and rubbed his hands. Up and down the road lights flickered in windows and reflected on newly fallen snow. Emile kept his eyes on the windows of his house, hoping for a reassuring silhouette. The kitchen light flared up. He strained toward the moving shadows. But it was not Alice he saw through the windows. Instead, the black barrels of machine guns poked out, pointing down the street and, to his utter horror, he could make out several Germans reclining at the kitchen table. They had taken over his house.

Oh my God, where were Alice and Evelyne? Were they still somewhere in Paron or had they been sent to a camp? Perhaps they were living with Louise. Emile hurtled down the road, careless of his safety, until he came to Louise's house, the plaque with the name *Villa des Oiseaux* still on the wall by the front door.

But once again no Alice. Only Germans.

He walked away sick with hopelessness, leaned against a wall where he vomited until his stomach was empty, raw and aching.

Alice was dead. He felt sure of that now. She was not well enough to withstand any sort of barbarous treatment and Evelyne was too young to survive. Emile walked back to the railway station, his face wet with tears.

There was no option. He would get out of France and go back to America, try to start a new life but always, always with the memory of his beloved Alice close to his heart.

CHAPTER 15

> The principal response of rural communities
> faced by repeated demands for meat, milk,
> eggs, potatoes, wheat, and oats
> was a sulky non-cooperation.
>
> - Robert Gildea

Emile Jochmans was being harassed by the *ravitaillment* officials who had been sent out to the rural areas to ensure delivery quotas and enforce price controls. It was up to them to make certain that farmers were dealing honestly with their produce, meaning that they were not holding back food required by the German occupiers.

The *gendarmerie* were also searching trucks and carts for illicit food and raiding isolated farms for produce held back from the official market. Then a ban was imposed on the making of farm butter and the private slaughter of livestock. Farmers grumbled and only complied with a resentful half-hearted co-operation. M. Jochmans was one such farmer and when he asked Alice if he could store some of his dried produce in her house, away from the greedy eyes of the *ravitaillment* officials, she had reluctantly agreed.

"Under the very noses of those bastards," he said, grinning like a naughty schoolboy. "Nowhere could be safer."

One afternoon when the soldiers had been called to a special parade, M. Jochmans inspected Alice's attic. But he shook his head. It was good in theory but would put Alice in danger. Not worth a few sacks of dried beans. After the inspection, M. Jochmans invited her to see his main hiding place.

They walked up the hill and behind the stables. All around them was evidence of a good and fertile summer. The fields were filled with gently waving grain. A farrow of new-born piglets scurried after the sow that ran squealing along the wall, snouting for tidbits. Over in the next field Alice could see the officer's horses, their coats gleaming in the sun. The warm weather seemed to soften the edges of occupation.

Behind the stables a small cave had been carved out of the hillside. M. Jochmans entered through the rough-cut doorway. He beckoned to Alice.

"Here," he said. "This is where we hide our food. It's also our wine cellar and we could use it as an air raid shelter if we need it."

"Do 'they' know about it?"

M. Jochmans shrugged and lit a candle. "They don't go past the wine cellar. Why do you think I have so few bottles left?"

Alice could see wine racks, now sadly depleted, and further back benches along the side walls. They walked past the benches and into the back of the small cave that curved like a dog's leg. She realized the main bulk of his hidden supplies were well beyond the stretch of candle light.

"Perfect, don't you think?" he asked with a devilish grin.

As she walked home Alice thought of the year since the soldiers had first come in such grey numbers, like rats overrunning a kitchen. She had changed from a girl play-acting her life to a woman with a child; hungry, fearful and with shoulders bowed by responsibilities. Was she the same person who had dressed up in silk and lace, flirted and laughed and had once been young enough to fall in love? Living under tyranny seemed to have diminished her, compressed her so that all joy had been squeezed out and all that was left was a grey mouse of a woman. She felt ancient in her broken shoes and sagging hemline. She had grown up and grown old in the space of a year.

Occupation became the only life she knew; the present a nightmare, the past a dream. The ubiquitous German soldiers tainted everything. They were everywhere. Marching, lounging, at play, sleeping. The *feld-grau* uniforms were all over the place; jackboots loud on the cobble stones and guttural voices the only sounds.

Billboards in the now-hated Gothic script covered the walls of public buildings. Everywhere one turned there seemed to be new instructions, new strictures, all starting with the word *"Verboten"*. Forbidden to listen to foreign radio – on pain of imprisonment. Forbidden to exceed the curfew – on pain of punishment. All windows to be closed during curfew. No one allowed to parade or take photographs outdoors or gather in crowds. Graffiti was also forbidden.

Vichy had its own set of strictures; no music, no dancing although they were not 'crimes', no one would be arrested for dancing.

But there was a huge variety of reasons for arrest; subversive remarks, any contravention of the curfew, listening to the radio, especially to the BBC (a somewhat futile restriction as only one per cent of the French population actually owned a radio). Displaying the French tricolor or singing the national anthem was naturally and expressly forbidden.

Anyone caught defacing a propaganda poster would be arrested and imprisoned. Worst of all, those who gave succor to Jews or refugees, the Resistance or Allied agents, or gave aid to an escaped prisoner or alien, would be executed.

The French answered with sullen animosity.

And then there was the setting of the clocks. Soon after the armistice the occupying forces had insisted on changing to 'international time'. Lulu and the Jochmans kept their clocks back sixty minutes to French time, whereas Alice was obliged to live by German time. She thought if she was really courageous she would have set her kitchen clock back to French time and defied the enemy within her walls. But there was Evelyne to think of.

Alice was in awe of Lulu who constantly broke the rules and seemed to get away with it. She said she knew someone in Sens with an illegal radio who listened to the news from the BBC, the British Broadcasting Corporation in London. Lulu passed on the news, making sure that those who were known collaborators did not know from where it had come. It was her part in the war effort, she said, keeping spirits high in such dark times. Alice liked Lulu all the more for that, liked the way she held her head high in spite of vicious disapproval of the villagers.

Lulu shrugged off the criticism. Servicing the Germans was just a job, nothing more, she said. She had flown the French flag from her window when France was free. Then came the English and she had flown the Union Jack alongside the Tricolor. Then the Germans came and she was damned if she was going to fly the swastika from her window, despite most of her clients being German. Lulu was staunch in her belief that the French would finally prevail over the enemy and that France would one day be free. Then she would once again fly the beautiful Tricolor from her window.

Alice wondered when occupation would end and if life could get any worse.

She was about to find out.

She sat in the kitchen with the official letter in her hands. It said that Emile's army pay would cease at the end of November. At first it did not make sense. She had heard other prisoners' wives mention they still received pay, albeit on a reduced scale.

And then it hit her. Emile was dead. Either that or in a prison camp in Germany, which would amount to the same thing. He seemed suddenly so far from her that the thread between them was almost at breaking point. He was dead. The very thought numbed her so that nothing else made sense. Not the oppression, not the soldiers in her house, not the everyday fear that rumbled constantly in the background.

It would never have occurred to her that he had escaped from the POW camp, had been reported as an escapee and that was why his army pay had ceased.

Her mind flew back to the first time they met. It was in New York and it was her twenty-third birthday. She had lived in the New York home of Louise Fromont and Jules Duxin for three years. There was a strict routine and Louise expected a full report on every moment she was out of the house. Why were you so long? Where did you go? Who were you with? Alice could not speak much English and that alone restricted any personal adventure, in spite of Louise's suspicions.

But things were about to change.

"What are you doing to your hair, girl? You look like a skivvy," Louise said.

Alice was about to say she looked like a skivvy because she was one. But caution caused the words to die before they were formed. She had always cut her own hair with a pair of kitchen scissors and washed it with laundry soap. It looked like it too. Her aunt had plenty of reason to criticize.

"I'll make an appointment for you to have your hair professionally cut," Louise said. "Just this once. I can't have you going around looking like that. What will people think of me?"

And so it was that Louise took Alice Guyonvernier, her ward and niece, to the Barberet Salon in Eighty-Fourth Street, the hair styling salon where Emile Pothron and Jacques Laffont worked evenings. It was Alice's first visit to a professional hair stylist and it would be a life-changing event.

Emile later told her he had not been keen to fill the appointment. Mme Fromont sounded impatient and demanding, so he'd passed the job on to Jacques who was older and a little more tolerant of difficult customers.

On a bitterly cold evening at the end of January 1927 Louise marched into the Barberet Salon. Behind her, like a timid shadow, walked Alice. Her hair was a mess but he instantly fell in love with the way her chin lifted and signaled a hidden bravado. Her nose was perfect, in Emile's eyes, a ski slope of a nose. Her eyes were clear and direct. Emile was irrevocably and eternally in love even before she sat down at his station.

And now he was dead. Alice crumpled the awful letter in her hands and tried to console herself. She would get through it, even if it was only for Evelyne.

All this would be over one day, all the humiliation and grief and fear; all the hunger and persecution. Perhaps they could go back to America where she and Emile had been so happy. She would show her daughter the places where they had lived and perhaps all the horror would fade and one day it would become only a half-remembered nightmare. These men who occupied her house would go home to their girlfriends, wives and children. They would continue their lives as if they had done no wrong, as if there had been nothing broken, nothing stained by their presence. One day it would be in the history books and students reading fat tomes in quiet libraries would never know the pain and loss and degradation that crouched between the dusty words.

She smoothed out the letter and read it again then placed it in her pocket. Numbly she picked up the bucket and force of habit directed her feet to the water pump. The handle fitted into her palm and she pressed down remembering that Emile's hand had pressed there before. She tried to remember what his hands felt like. Were they strong, sturdy and reliable? Were they the hands of one who had said he would return but now would never come back?

... *un* ... *deux* ... *trois* ... Emile ... Emile ... *quatre* ... *cinq*. It paid to count, the numbers slipping past her so that she did not have to think ... Emile, Emile.

"When can I see you again?" he had whispered as he cut her hair. She had been too afraid to say anything but he had interpreted the nervous glance she directed towards her aunt.

"Ah, so we'll have to be careful," he had said and her heart flooded with delighted anticipation.

Now it was over and she would be alone for the rest of her life. It did not bear thinking of. When the water bucket was full she carried it to the kitchen. The men sat round the table, laughing and smoking. Evelyne watched hungrily from a corner as they ate from a small bag of oranges, juice dripping from their chins, their fingers glistening. You sick bastards, Alice thought. You rob us of everything.

CHAPTER 16

Childhood is measured out by sounds
and smells and sights, before the
dark hour of reason grows.
- John Betjeman

Evelyne Claudette Pothron was a child born of war. Her birth in June 1939 occurred just before her father's call-up and her babyhood was spent without him. Her first conscious experiences were of deprivation, although at the time it was as natural as the sun coming up. She had had her first birthday just days before the Germans arrived and from that moment their jackbooted steps thundered through her small world.

She was rather curious about these monsters in their grey-green uniforms. They were so enormous that it seemed she was more acquainted with their shiny boots than with their faces. They all dressed in the same clothes so that she sometimes confused the good ones with the bad. Some chose to ignore her while others bent down to her, smiled and chucked her under the chin or rumpled her curls. It was at these rare moments that *Maman* would swing her up and away from their rough hands. At first it puzzled her and then, through *Maman's* fear, she too learned to be afraid.

They also made very loud noises, these giants, not meant to scare her, but they did. Sometimes there was gunfire, stuttering through the air from the forest above the village and she knew it was them by the way *Maman* flinched. Then the snarling of motorbikes and wagons that roared past their house, the stomp of marching feet and the shouts of orders outside in the long sun-rinsed street where she never went without *Maman*. Those noises were the background to her life, ones she could not identify as being dangerous, only strident and sudden. The worst were the inside noises, the songs, the slapping down of cards on the kitchen table and the loud laughter that did not seem at all like happy sounds.

It was a very solitary life for a child. *Tante* Louise and *oncle* Jules lived down the road, but they were not much fun to visit. *Oncle* Jules' whiskers tickled and his fingers were rough but *Maman* snatched her away whenever he bent down to hug her. But to compensate there was the farm. Evelyne loved the enormous animals that looked over the fence and nuzzled her when she got close. The fat ungainly pigs in the yard and the old dog with a grey muzzle that allowed her to sit close enough to see into his milky eyes. The sinuous black cat that was allowed in the kitchen and no further, although she found out later that Emilienne carried her to bed each evening. She would remember those animals and love them forever.

Of course there was the Jochmans' kitchen, an exciting place where other children played and fought and cried. It was filled with movement and sound and smells that forever afterwards meant safety. Her small life included all these she thought of as her family, who fussed over her, pulled at her clothes and affectionately rubbed her back when she cried.

She had no toys to play with or much else to satisfy her growing curiosity about the world. *Maman* tried her best, entertaining her when she could, like the game of pumping water.

"Come now," *Maman* would call. "Say it after me ... *un, deux, trois.*" Up and down went the handle of the pump, *Maman's* slim hand holding the bucket and the water sloshing clear and bubbly. Evelyne's childish voice repeated the numbers ... *un* ... *deux* ... *trois.* Before she was two years old Evelyne had learned her numbers at the water pump.

Her closest friends were the animals that seemed to wander into her life and just as quickly disappear. There was a hutch of rabbits whose pink furry ears were soft as silk. The rabbits were docile enough for her to wheel around in her toy wheelbarrow but, for

Evelyne in the garden at Paron

157

some reason, they did not stay around long enough to become really tame. Evelyne sometimes wondered where the rabbits went.

Red-feathered chickens clucked and scratched under the trees in their back yard. They ran when Evelyne tried to play with them but they were fun, especially when she had the proud pleasure of showing *Maman* where they had secretly hidden an egg for her to find.

At one stage they had a small goat that *Maman* secretly called Adolf. She did not understand that because there was a picture of Adolf in the kitchen that the soldiers had stuck to the wall and he did not look a bit like the goat in the garden. Besides, their goat was a lady. *Maman* had said so when she got milk out of its titties.

She had another secret, one she did not tell *Maman*. She had a new friend, one that lived under the stairs leading to the attic. It had come out to make friends with her, its long whiskers twitching in the cold morning air. It shot away whenever there were loud footsteps on the stairs. But Evelyne had managed to coax it out again by feeding it a small piece of food. Once she fed it with a piece of her morning bread and watched with pleasure as it delicately took the morsel in its paws and nibbled politely. She was delighted when it came closer and was sad when it shot back into the attic through a hole in the skirting board, its long pink tail trembling. It all came to an end when *Maman* walked up the stairs and gave a loud shriek and one of the giants ran up. *Maman* had gone all funny and the giant had just laughed and said he would catch the horrible rat and wring its neck. Evelyne cried and that was the last time she saw her friendly rat. But she noticed the attic door was not left open any more. Now it had a big padlock on it and *Maman* said it was to keep the rats out.

Evelyne, Skippy and friends

"Evelyne, what do you think you're doing?" *Maman* called. "Go outside right this minute and play in the garden."

Evelyne heard that far too often and while she loved to play in the sun-splashed garden among the trees and vegetables growing in their little beds, she always suspected she was being sent out for a reason. And that reason, she only vaguely understood, was her mother's distress.

There were a few of the giants that *Maman* definitely did not like, and so Evelyne did not like them either. The nice ones sang her songs in a strange language that seemed to come from the back of their throats and sometimes even gave her a piece of fruit. It was from the others that *Maman* protected her with the order to 'go outside and play'.

It was on one of her 'sent-out' times that she discovered the kittens. The outhouse door was always closed and the hasp and staple too high for her to reach. But in the far corner of the garden stood another shed on crumbly foundations. She could creep into it through the broken door and play. It was here that Evelyne found a litter of feral kittens under a shelf. She knelt down to watch them sleep. They were so small, their eyes tightly closed. She picked one up and cradled it in her hands.

Evelyne ran to the house, up the stairs and through the kitchen door. "*Maman, Maman,*" she called, her voice high with excitement. "Look, look."

"*Was ist?*" Large rough hands took hold of the kitten. It hissed and struggled against the calluses and broken nails. "*Eine katze.*"

Laughter and another giant took the kitten by the tail. It squealed in terror. "*Eine schmutzige katze.*"

Evelyne stamped her foot. "*Non, non.* It's not dirty. You dirty."

The giant swung the kitten round and round by its tail, a small gray screeching smudge of claws and wet fur. "*Läast spiel ein spiel.*"

"*Futball?*"

There was raucous laughter as the helpless kitten swung to and fro. Evelyne began to scream.

"*Geben sie es zurück,*" said one of the giants, the one who had once given her a small piece of chocolate. He gently took the kitten and gave it back to Evelyne. In his halting French he told her to go and put it back with its mother. She was only too pleased to get out of the kitchen and back to the shed. It was the last time she showed any of her prizes to the giants.

And, of course, there was Skippy who made a great playmate and confidante. He had fully recovered from the amateur surgery skills of his owner and was now able to join in Evelyne's games. By turns he was a carriage bearer, an aide de camp, a baby in a stroller with an old bonnet on his head. They were inseparable. *Maman* had only to see the wagging tail or the white furry ball of a sleeping Skippy to know where Evelyne was.

The one time when Skippy was not around Evelyne almost caused an international scene. It was early in the morning when *Maman* thought it too cold for Evelyne to accompany her to the water pump.

"Now you wait in the kitchen where it's warm," *Maman* had said. "Sit still and don't bother the soldiers."

She knew why *Maman* did not take her out in the cold. She had grown out of her shoes and *Maman* had to take a knife and cut through the front so that her toes peeped through and got wet in the snow. Still, it was boring having to wait in the kitchen with all the soldiers asleep on the floor.

She decided that particular morning to spend the time examining the men, looking at the ones who drooled onto their greatcoats or made funny snoring noises. When she grew tired of that she devised a new game to play. She began skipping around, jumping over the soldier's boots that were neatly placed in rows at the end of their straw pallets.

"Un." She jumped over the first pair.

"Deux." Over the next pair, careful that she did not touch the boots for then she would have to start the game all over again.

"Trois."

And that was when *Maman* entered the kitchen, gave a small shriek and snatched her up.

"The only time we are safe, little Madame, is when they're asleep. Don't ever wake them up, do you hear me?"

Evelyne could feel *Maman's* heart beating fast.

CHAPTER 17

> Everything can be taken from a man but one
> thing: the last of the human freedoms –
> to choose one's attitude in any given set
> of circumstances ...
>
>   - Viktor Frankl

On the return journey to Paris, Emile's thoughts were suicidal. What had they done to Alice and the baby? Where were they? Were they dead? Yes, they must be.

He was hungry, tired and fearful, so thinking the worst came easily. His body started to shake. Soon his teeth were chattering, his skin pasty and moist with shock. Passengers around him looked alarmed.

"Are you ill, Monsieur?"

"*Non, non. Merci.*"

No, not ill, but to Emile it felt like the end of the world. He tried to hang on to his sanity, looked around him, noting the changes, keeping his mind on anything but his lost family. He had not witnessed the swift deterioration of life in France. Now it seemed to be everywhere, or perhaps it was merely a reflection of his inner wasteland.

After only six months of occupation, people around him looked shabby, their faces weathered by constant anxiety and hunger. From the train window he noticed there were no private vehicles on the roads, only some business trucks and a great many German transporters moving men and equipment.

But Alice tugged at his thoughts. If she were alive then where could she be? He thought of trying to find her. But how? There were no telephones and the postal service was in a shambles with censorship by the Germans and the *gendarmes*. Telegrams were still a possibility but who could he contact? He was not the only person who had lost touch with family, but that knowledge did nothing to lighten his mood of desperation.

Then he remembered what he had said to Alice. 'If the worst happens, then go to Nice.' Had she done so? Had they left Paron? But how could she get to Nice? By train? Possibly. The Citroën! No, she could not drive. There was a bitter irony in the thought of the Citroën sitting in their garage and Alice stranded because she could not drive. He cursed himself for not having taught her. Was the auto still there or had it been confiscated? He had not thought to check. He could have spent a few minutes peering through the crack between door and jamb, but he had not. He had been stupid. But nothing seemed to matter once he had looked into the kitchen and seen it filled with those damned jackbooted Nazis chattering like baboons with cigarettes hanging from their evil mouths.

Perhaps it was his air of brash indifference that got him through the turnstile at the Bercy railway station in Paris and the German guards checking papers. He walked through with a noisy group of men and did not even try to look inconspicuous. He no longer cared.

He took the Metro to the area where he had met the one-legged man and from there finally found his way back to the heavy carriage doors and into the courtyard. The helpers knew where he had been and his grey face told them the story. They patted him clumsily on the back and put a lighted cigarette into his fingers. Later, he lay on the bed in the cellar with only a candle for company. They did not trouble him, merely allowed him to work through his grief. A few days waiting for a new travel document and food coupons that arrived together with several hundred francs and he was ready to move out again.

"Go to our contact, no one else. Don't try to get over on your own. It's too dangerous. Our man on the border will know who to trust. We hear some of the guides are scoundrels. They charge the earth, take you to the demarcation line and then leave you. On top of that there are Nazis patrols with dogs. We've heard they take pleasure in wounding an escapee and then letting the dogs have some fun."

"Surely that's just a rumor? People just aren't that cruel," Emile protested.

The man merely shrugged.

Emile wondered why they did it; put their lives at risk for a stranger. When he asked, the man smiled.

"We have to do something. We can't let them win."

Emile left a few days later. He walked to *Gare d'Austerlitz* from where he caught a southbound train. As instructed by the men in Paris, he would go some of the way by train. He had been warned it was a little risky as inspectors constantly checked for suspect documents. After that he would have to walk but, he had been assured, it would be fairly safe as long as he kept off the main roads. The contact near Montluçon knew and trusted the *passeurs* who would get him across the demarcation line and into Vichy France. Once on the other side, the men said, it would be easier to make his way south. There would be no Germans and the French *gendarmes* often looked the other way.

The Paris men had been vague about his chances after the demarcation line. None of them had travelled this route and knew no one except the man to whom Emile had been directed. It was not good to know too much, they said.

Emile understood the necessity of compartmentalizing the escape route. Captain Delavierre had explained how easy it would be for the Germans to infiltrate and roll up a whole line of helpers. When a helper landed in German hands they were inevitably tortured, executed or sent to a concentration camp – but not before they had told everything they knew. If he or she could hold out for forty-eight hours, Delavierre had surmised, then the others would have a chance, a small one but in most cases that was all they needed to melt away and begin again somewhere else.

Emile would also have to be careful about asking questions; no names, no addresses and absolutely nothing in writing. He promised himself he would be like the three monkeys; see nothing, hear nothing, say nothing. He owed it to the people who had given so much; food, accommodation and money when they had so little and who asked for nothing in return. Each one had put their lives, and those of their loved ones, on the line for a stranger. Emile wondered how he could ever repay such courage.

At *Gare d'Austerlitz* he once again sidled, as part of the working throng, through the ticket barricade and past the *gendarmes.* An inspector gave his papers a cursory look and handed them back. He boarded and sat down on one of the wooden seats as the train strained out of the station before picking up speed. Emile wondered if he should pretend to sleep. He thought it would save him from having to offer his illicit credentials for inspection. It would also prevent him having to participate in any conversation. He did not feel up to inventing the usual banter with which working men passed the time. His mind was still full of the scene he had witnessed in Paron; the machine guns, the German soldiers, while Alice's absence screamed at him through the open window. He still needed to process the information and try to make sense of it.

He looked at the towns and fields as the train clattered past and wondered if he might have been safer on the road. Being in a confined space meant he had little chance of escape if his documents did not pass scrutiny. The train filled and emptied, filled again. From time to time, groups of German soldiers pushed their way in, carrying their rifles carelessly over their shoulders. Other passengers were giving them a wide berth but Emile thought that being in the middle of the group would be the safest place, like being in the eye of a storm, calm and untouchable. He got up and moved towards them. Casually, he insinuated himself into their midst. When the moment of ticket inspection finally came it must have seemed as if he was with the soldiers. The inspector did no more than shrug his shoulders and walk on, examining other papers on the way.

The bridge over the Loire had been repaired and the train rumbled over wooden trestles and towards the town of Nevers. Emile remembered what had worked when he went to Paron and so he pushed his way to the end of the carriage where he waited for the train to slow as it entered the station. When it did, he jumped down and walked along the track until he came to the town.

He went to a small café east of the railway station where he ordered a meal. He had to remind himself to eat like a European. Ten years in America had softened many of his Continental habits and he now ate as Americans did; cutting up his food and then eating with only a fork in his hand instead of using knife and fork together as the Europeans did. After his dinner Emile registered at the front desk of a nearby hotel, the concierge writing his new name on the *fiche*, the official card index, and pointing up the stairs to a room on the right. Emile checked the window. It looked out on a small courtyard and there was a fire escape just below the window sill. An escape route if needed. The curtains and wallpaper were faded. A small wardrobe gave off the musty odor of long-gone overcoats. A hand basin stood on a dresser with a jug of water. Emile washed his face and hands and fell onto the bed and was soon asleep.

Early morning Nevers was filled with German soldiers patrolling the streets, passing in trucks, with dogs held on tight leather leashes. He remembered how he and the members of his unit had thought they would be safe south of the Loire. They had drastically underestimated the German advance.

He began to walk out of the city hoping for a lift. It was not long in coming. The truck was driven by a taciturn old man in a butcher's apron whose pipe was stuffed with something other than tobacco. Emile asked him about his business. Was it hard to get gas for his truck? The man merely nodded. Was he able to get supplies of meat? Again the man only nodded. Was the system of food coupons working? The man shrugged. Emile belatedly realized he had given himself away by asking questions that were naïve in the extreme. The butcher would know he was an escapee. Oh God! How stupid!

He slumped in the seat and allowed the silence to build between them. The butcher dropped him at the side of the road well beyond the outskirts of town and Emile began to walk, hoping the old man would decide to mind his own business.

Once he heard a rumble and instinctively dove behind a hedge. Through the snow-coated leaves he watched as truck after laden truck, each followed by an auto filled with armed guards, passed him and sped north. He had been so lost in thought that he had only heard their approach at the last moment. He felt sick with fright so he made his way into a copse of trees and lay down until composure allowed him to slip into a light doze.

When it began to get dark, he started to walk again until he spotted a few lights in the distance. As he got closer he heard the barking of farm dogs. Cutting through a snowy field he made his way to a small hay-filled barn a short distance from the main house. He creaked open the barn door and climbed into the sweet-smelling bales of hay where he snuggled down to sleep. A cold breeze flurried the snow outside but Emile felt safe and his sleep was deep and satisfying.

Through the morning mist Emile saw the farmer and his dogs trudging towards the barn. He scrambled up, dusted off his trousers and pulled the straw from his hair. In a few moments he would either be marching to the nearest *gendarmerie* or he was about to be offered breakfast. His second guess was the right one.

The kitchen was warm and the table set for three. The farmer's wife placed a plate of food in front of him.

"Merci," he said. *"Merci beaucoup."* Thank you very much.

Emile was not sure how much to reveal. He belatedly remembered the words of advice given him by Delavierre – say as little as possible and ask no questions. Especially stupid ones he thought, remembering his *faux pas* the day before. He applied himself to the job in hand, making short shrift of breakfast. Over a bowl of steaming milk, in which pieces of bread floated like islands, Emile asked if the farmer knew the blacksmith.

He nodded.

After the meal the farmer walked with him to the edge of his property and then pointed out the way. He told Emile of the two minor roads he would need to cross before he came to the blacksmith's home. He warned him not to speak to anyone as there were collaborators in the area, people who would betray a stranger as quickly as looking at them. The farmer pressed a small parcel of bread and cheese into Emile's hand before he walked away.

The blacksmith's house was set back a little way from the road and surrounded by snow covered fields. Emile hid in a shallow ditch on the side of the road until night came, pulling with it a star-filled sky that glistened on the snow like a thousand diamonds. Once the sun had set, Emile thought it safe to risk knocking on the front door. It opened a crack, spilling light onto the frozen path. A wizened face peered out.

"I've come from Paris," he said. "I was told to find the blacksmith."

The expression on the old face did not change. "Go away," it said. Emile stuck his foot in the door as it began to close. "Tell him I've come from Paris."

"You better tell him yourself," the face said and the door opened wide enough for him to slip through. A small woman dressed in rusty black pointed to the back of the house and to a room filled with light and soft voices that stilled as he walked in.

"Another one," someone said, the accent pure Oxford. "By Jove, jolly good show."

The babble of voices began again and one man detached himself from the crowd, took Emile by the arm and led him out into the passage.

"Are you the blacksmith?" Emile asked.

The man nodded. "Who sent you?"

Emile explained about the men in Paris. He showed his documents, which the blacksmith studied intently. It seemed to do the trick. The man's face broke into a smile and he took Emile's hand and pumped it.

"Welcome," he said. "Come in and share some wine with us. Have you eaten?"

Emile shook his head. "Who are these people?"

"They are all in the same boat as you, *mon ami*. All want to get through the border and into free France."

"When do we leave?"

The man shrugged. "When the *passeurs* get here."

Emile handed over the four hundred francs needed to cover payment to the guides. The blacksmith assured him they knew the area, knew where the dangers lay and the safest place to cross the demarcation line. He offered Emile a chunk of bread and cheese and a glass of wine which he held up as a toast.

The demarcation line was now so close Emile could almost taste freedom.

CHAPTER 18

There are in the life of a nation times that wound
the memory and the idea one has of one's country. It
is difficult to talk about such things ...
That day, France, the cradle of Enlightenment
and human rights, a safe haven for the oppressed,
committed an unforgiveable sin.
Breaking its word, it delivered those it should
protect to their executioners.

- Jacques Chirac
President, France 1995 – 2007

Marshal Pétain blamed the defeat of France on
'leftists', Communists, trade unionists, civil
libertarians, Freemasons and, above all, Jews, who, he
said, were particularly prone to immorality. Fault
cannot be so simply apportioned, but the result of
Pétain's name-calling and finger-pointing became
evident soon after the Armistice in 1940 when a
seedy sort of contamination, one built of despair and
humiliation, permeated life in France. It was
someone else's fault, it had to be, and the Jews were,
once again, the scapegoats.

France's traditional fairness, justice and
compassion were swept aside in the desolation of
defeat. It was as if France had lost its moral compass
and the consequences would be calamitous.

Believing it had no option, the Vichy government
forged close links with what has proved to be the one
of the most evil regimes in modern history. The mass
of French people adored Pétain, the hero of the Great

War. They saw him as their savior – and why not? It appeared as if he had single-handedly saved France from the worst ravages of war, not once but twice. They were wrong, of course. Worse was yet to come but most people accepted his dictatorial powers and followed his collaborationist urgings through necessity, moral laxity or just plain fear.

On 3 October 1940, barely a month after taking office, the Vichy government, under the leadership of Pétain, produced the infamous *Statut des Juifs,* Statute on Jews. It was a set of discriminatory laws that declared Jews to be of a lower class and deprived them of their French citizenship. They were excluded from certain professions, such as teaching, the media, law and medicine. It also declared the exclusion of Jews from commerce and industry. In a short time, more than half of all French Jews were deprived of their means of livelihood. Vichy was willing to participate in and, indeed, exceeded Hitler's plan for total extermination. Later, Pétain made the excuse that it was 'them or us'. He may have been right. History is no crystal ball but, in hindsight, the French would probably have preferred glory to humiliation.

An example of officialdom's co-operation with Hitler's mechanism of evil took place on 14 May 1941 when the French police arrested nearly 4,000 Jewish men and placed them in the Paris Winter Velodrome (*Vélodrome d'Hiver*) situated on the corner of *boulevard de Grenelle* and *rue Nélaton* in the 15th *arrondisement* near the Eiffel Tower. Later they were transferred to the suburb of Drancy, which had been turned into a transit camp, run not by the Germans but by the French police. From there these Jews would eventually be transported to Auschwitz.

Sens and Paron were not exempt from the 'Jewish Problem' as the Germans called it. Alice knew of several Jewish families living in the area. She had seen them walking along the streets or in the shops buying whatever food they could afford. As they had no ration cards this was a particularly futile exercise. Some looked furtive, watching for strangers in raincoats and fedoras – the uniform of the Gestapo – but most went about their affairs with as much quiet dignity as they could muster. This was not yet the time of enforced wearing of the yellow star – that would only come in June 1942 – but Alice sensed their difference as if they already had the Star of David pinned to their coats. Their fear was palpable and it stood out beyond any enforced label.

Alice staunchly believed the French would look after their own, no matter their religion. And those refugees who had sought sanctuary would also be cared for. France was the bastion of liberty, equality and fraternity, the ideals fought for in the Revolution of 1789, and they would not be given up in a hurry. It was a caring nation and those who sought refuge within its borders would be safe. It was one of the things she loved about France; its compassion. The Jews of Paron would be safe, she was sure of it.

The ideals of the Revolution were her ideals. They were the ideals of France and she loved it, all of it; the language that rolled off her tongue like a river over washed pebbles, the vineyards and purple lavender, the fussy old men in berets playing *petanque*, fierce wine and great wheels of cheese maturing in dusty storehouses. She even loved the elegant women who minced along the cobbled streets of Paris. And, of course, she loved Emile. To her, Emile was the epitome of France; his determined mouth, his small precise body and his caring nature. His eyes, she remembered, were the color of the Seine.

But Emile was no more. She was pierced with a longing so fierce that she folded over clutching at her stomach, weakened by its awful power.

Alice tried to draw strength from the stalwart women around her. They, too, had lost someone; a father, a son, a husband. She found herself admiring them - even those who spoke against her - clothed in whatever rags were left of their faded wardrobes, clinging at their dignity as they held their families and their country together. They were part of a great throng of the indomitable, the survivors and the traditional home keepers who had reshaped their lives and taken on roles for which they were untrained and unsuited. They had succeeded magnificently and would, Alice believed, play a key role in the survival of France as a nation.

They hid their grief and just got on with it, she thought. I'll do the same. I'll come through this. We all will. At heart people are good. They had to be or life was not worth the effort.

When her strength failed Lulu was there to console her. She held Alice in her arms as the young woman wept for her husband, wept that he would never see his daughter grow up.

"Come, *ma cherie*. We'll take a walk. It'll clear your head," Lulu said one day after Alice had collapsed in her arms.

They took Evelyne down to the River Yonne and stood watching the barges move slowly past carrying tarpaulin-shrouded war equipment from Germany. Evelyne scurried around making a cairn of stones gathered from the bank of the river and chatting to Skippy who pranced beside her.

"Someone should blow that lot up," Alice said bitterly.

175

Lulu dragged on her cigarette and flicked the ash off with a ballerina hand. "I agree but we'll have to organize ourselves if we want to make a difference. Trouble is most people are too afraid."

"The soldiers all talk about the thousand-year Reich, so I suppose people feel they'll never be free again," said Alice. "It gives them the excuse they need to do nothing."

Lulu laughed. "Some people don't need an excuse. It's all too sad. France used to be the center of Western civilization, where all the great artists came to create. We had a responsibility to the world to keep the flame of civilization alive and we failed. How could we have let it all slip so easily from our grasp?"

"You speak so well, Lulu, you should have been a politician."

Lulu let out a hoot of laughter. "A politician? Let me tell you, young lady. I wouldn't lower myself to be a politician."

Alice giggled at the thought. It was hilarious. She began to laugh, a rich bellowing sound and soon Lulu joined her. They laughed until their sides ached and their eyes watered. And still they laughed, a healing clamor. Soon they were on the hard ground where they kicked their legs up and hooted and shrieked their mirth.

Eventually, Alice gained a modicum of sobriety. "Perhaps you're right," she said. "There is nothing lower."

Lulu sat up, threw her cigarette down and ground it out with her elegant shoe. "How did we allow this to happen?" she asked when their laughter had ended. "Where are our heroes?"

"We better not let anyone hear us talking like that. We'll be branded as *résistants*."

Lulu's eyebrows shot up. "And we don't want that, do we!"

"Are you being sarcastic?"

"Perhaps not," said Lulu quietly. "But we must do something for France, for freedom."

"Anyway," Alice said, hauling Evelyne onto her hip. "You're right. Better to keep our opinions to ourselves."

It was the Jewish business that reminded Alice of their conversation.

She had been aware of anti-Semitism in America but it had not really penetrated the small world that revolved around her and Emile. Yes, she had made dresses for Jewish women and Emile had styled their hair, but why were they considered different from anyone else? They smiled, worked hard and paid their way, made love, cared for their children. So, what was the problem?

Then things in Sens and Paron took an ugly turn. First, a couple of Jewish businesses in Sens were targeted. Nothing much; just a tobacconist and a small jeweler in a side street near the river; first looted then burned.

Then, in June, the *gendarmes* went to the houses. They took away the tobacconist, his wife and children, the jeweler and his aged mother. They were being "relocated" the neighbors were told. Nothing sinister – just "relocation".

Early one morning Alice heard a commotion in the street. As she peeped through the net curtain at her window she saw people running, scattering like ants from an overturned nest, some rushing towards the river. Shouts and rifle shots tore at the air. Down the street a canvas-covered truck moved slowly. A *gendarme* was driving but several German soldiers clung to the sides, rifles banging against their thighs. In the back of the truck, guarded by two local *gendarmes,* Alice saw the white-faced families she had only known in passing. A few were crying or looking angry but mostly their faces had the blank look worn by those who understood the requirements of martyrdom.

Ahead of the truck, by accident or design, a small handcart had overturned, spilling its contents across the road. The guards jumped off the truck and walked to the front, haranguing people who were scooping up the spilled goods. In and out of the chaos children ran, shouting, snatching up whatever they could. It was then Alice saw Lulu run to the back of the truck.

"Quick," she called. "The children."

A small boy was handed out to Lulu's waiting arms.

"Madame," a voice implored her. "My girls."

"Where?"

They had to hurry. The commotion was subsiding. Soon the truck would pull away.

"Madame Gilbert has my baby. The girls are in school, Madame. Hélène and Jacqueline."

The driver put the truck into gear and drove away. Lulu disappeared through an open door.

Long after the truck had left Paron and its load of Jews pushed into cattle trucks at the Sens railway station, a few muddied creatures crept from the reeds on the bank of the river and from the empty houses near the old railroad. They were quickly hustled into village houses. Doors closed behind them and shutters were slammed across windows.

The full and dreadful extent of Nazi extermination was not yet known, but there was a gut feel, an adumbration in the air, a darkening of the spirit that told of evil events. Some of the people of Paron heard the dirge singing on the wind and had responded.

Lulu stood near the school under the dappled shade of a plane tree. The bell rang for the end of classes and children's voices, sweet as ripe cherries, floated towards her through the dusty afternoon air. She stood watching until the two girls walked out. Emilienne, the farmer's daughter, walked with them. Hélène held onto the hand of her sister who skipped on dainty feet beside her. Each carried their school books in a leather satchel on their backs. They were smiling.

Much later Alice asked Lulu. "*Où sont les enfants?*" Where are the children?
Lulu looked blank and then smiled.
"*Quels enfants?*" What children?
Alice did not ask again.

CHAPTER 19

ZEUC ENZUNAGO ERYOTZEA DAVO AZCAZU URRAGO
(When you hear me, you will be closer to death)
- Inscription on the bells of the Church of Asunción, Gernika (Guernica)

In the blacksmith's back room, a hushed voice reminded them it was Christmas Day, and they were far from home. It was a tense twenty-four hours for Emile, sitting quietly with seven other equally tense young men.

They were dressed in what looked like cast-off clothes; baggy trousers and coats threadbare at the elbows. Underneath Emile could see the hint and shape of Allied uniforms. Each one had the ubiquitous French beret on his head, although on most it sat like a forest mushroom. Emile decided that only a true Frenchman could wear a beret with panache and he pulled on his so that it sat at a more Continental angle.

A meal of soup, bread and cheese was brought to them by the wizened old crone. Afterwards they were allowed outside, in ones and twos, to stretch their legs or find a tree behind which to urinate.

"No speaking," the blacksmith said. "Germans up there, yes?" He thumbed the near horizon. He explained their voices would carry in the still air. It was safer to be silent.

Just before midnight the two *passeurs* arrived and the blacksmith gave them last minute instructions. Walk in single file, no talking and watch for hand signals. If discovered they were to run, scattering so that at least some would have a chance of coming out alive. There were guards, he said, with dogs and the dogs can smell a man at a great distance, especially a fearful one. Emile was disheartened by the pessimism. It was only later he realized the blacksmith was just being realistic.

After a last handshake, they finally set off in single file as they'd been instructed. The moon was obscured by a flurry of cloud, but at least there was no new snow and there would be no tracks for the Germans to follow. At first, they walked along a narrow path between dripping hedges. Then they cut through a fallow field, tripping and cursing under their breath as they stumbled over the rough terrain. They could hear the voices of German guards and their dogs barking but not yet the baying of a blood-lust animal. In the still night air, sound was deceptive and they did not know how near or far away the dogs were. They plodded on as if the Germans were nearby. Once the lead *passeur* held up his hand and they crouched on the iron-cold ground until he was satisfied the movement he had seen was only a stray sheep.

After walking for two hours over empty fields, through ditches filled with dirty snow and across narrow roads, they finally came to a fence. Again, the hand signal.

They crouched down waiting.

Minutes passed.

They listened for the stomp of boots and the snuffle of dogs, knowing all the while that to be discovered now would be fatal. Finally the lead-*passeur* stood up, pulled the fence down and, one by one, the men clambered over it.

"Gentlemen," he said. "You are now in *la zone libre*."

The men would have cheered had they not been so cold and frightened, had they not been so close to the enemy. They were taken by one of the guides in one direction and two civilians walked off in another. Emile was left with the last guide.

"Now what?" he asked.

"Now, you come with me. I'll take you to a safe house for the night. Then you go by bicycle into Montluçon. After that you're on your own."

This time the farmer at the safe house did not acknowledge him. All he did was show Emile to a room under the house, light a candle for him and close the door. The room was sparse. There was a narrow bed and an empty wardrobe. On a table covered by an old lace cloth a plate of bread and paté had been laid out with a small carafe of wine. Emile assumed this was his supper. In the corner a forlorn bicycle was held together with wire, a label announced an address where he was to deposit it the next day. Obviously the farmer and his family wanted as little contact with him as possible.

The bed was hard. The blanket smelt as if the farmer had just taken it off the back of a horse. Never mind, for the moment he was safe and warm. Emile ate the supper and then fell onto the bed. He was asleep almost before his head hit the pillow.

The next morning he rode the rickety bicycle into Montluçon. He had a small parcel of food, left by the taciturn farmer and, on a hill outside the town, he sat under a tree to eat and smoke a cigarette while he thought about what to do next. He had transport and, with luck, could find enough food to survive. Or he could find work in the Dunlop factory as his forged documents indicated.

A sign pointed the way. He cycled along the road until he could see the Dunlop tire factory through the trees. To his utter horror he saw a large number of German trucks loaded with new tires leaving through the gates. Other German trucks, their grey-green paint dull in the morning light, were driving towards the factory. This did not feel right. Montluçon and the Dunlop factory were in the free zone and yet it was obvious the Germans were exploiting the synthetic rubber factory for their vehicles and aircraft.

Bloody cheek, Emile thought angrily. Was this Pétain's doing? Was this part of the Armistice agreement? He doubted it, and wondered if there was somebody he could tell about this, someone who would come over and bomb the hell out of the factory.

It was a good place to keep well clear of, he thought. There would be tight security with the Germans always on the lookout for subversives, saboteurs and escaped POWs with false papers. He could not, dare not, go anywhere near the place.

Emile lay watching the empty trucks lined up in front of what looked like storerooms the size of aircraft hangars. He counted the warehouses, drew in his mind a detailed sketch of the layout and estimated the length and width, the angles to other buildings. He had to remember it all. It would not be wise, he knew, to put anything on paper. If he were found to have any sort of plan on him he would automatically be branded a spy and shot. He'd heard talk in the blacksmith's house. The guides had also advised them to steer clear of any military installations – just in case. He lay there on the snow counting trucks arriving and trucks leaving.

And it was at this point that Emile Pothron disappeared.

CHAPTER 20

They were not human. This Nazi thing seemed to have just taken them over and turned them into something that I [Nancy Wake] had not thought humanly possible.

-   Peter Fitzsimons

Although the Germans were triumphant throughout Europe and their u-boats controlled the Atlantic, the September 1940 date for the invasion of England had come and gone.

That little country, alone against Hitler's might, hung on to freedom by its fingernails even though London had been bombed almost out of existence and England was slowly being starved into submission. America was willing to help with food and armaments but still it remained neutral.

The situation seemed hopeless.

Then Hitler made a mistake, one that would eventually lead to his downfall. On 22 June 1941, he opened a second front on the Russian border. He should have taken note of the French Emperor Napoleon's 1812 defeat on the winter plains of Russia, a country that had the population numbers and the weather on its side. Hitler was about to learn the hard way.

But on that hot summer day in early July the soldiers occupying Alice's house in Paron were celebrating. A group had gathered in her kitchen, singing and drinking beer. Amid the patriotic songs and strident laughter they listened to radio reports of their panzer divisions cutting a swath of destruction over a two thousand mile front from the Baltic to the Black Sea.

The announcer's voice shrieked. "Nothing will stop our glorious army from capturing Moscow."

A chorus of drunken voices yelled agreement.

"Soon the German Army will control all of Russia's oil fields, industrial complexes and her vast fertile fields. Nothing will stand in the way as our Wehrmacht rolls through Russia, crushing everything before it."

The men in Alice's house were increasingly raucous and jovial. The successes on the Eastern Front were their successes. They knew the Luftwaffe was in command of the sky. They had the weapons, the discipline and the determination. It was going to be a rout.

In spite of its overwhelming numbers, the Russian Army was weak. Stalin had purged every senior military man above lieutenant and had left his Army, Navy and Air Force incapable of withstanding the supremacy of the Germans.

Nothing but a miracle could stop the Germans from capturing Moscow.

A hot day of jubilation stretched into a stifling twilight and still they celebrated. Outside the day turned from blue to purple and then to a velvety black as the sun set. In the clear sky, a multitude of stars seemed to burn holes in the canopy above. And still they rejoiced.

At Alice's kitchen table they thumped their beer mugs, beating out a rhythm of triumph.

"Moskau! Moskau! Moskau!"

Some of the men started singing the national anthem:

Deutschland, Deutschland über alles,
Über alles in der Welt,
Germany, Germany, above everything,
Above everything in the world,

Alice had given up the kitchen to the men and taken refuge in her bedroom. In her absence they brought in two stolen geese, which they slaughtered on the once-clean floor. Feathers scattered under their feet, a pile of warm steaming intestines lay in a corner, potato peels followed. Soon the aroma of roasted duck and baked potatoes filled the house. They ate in guttural good humor, chins and fingers glistening with hot fat.

Another keg of beer.

Someone bashed the spigot in and foam slopped onto the floor.

Later who could say what had prompted them? Who was the first to suggest further entertainment? Alice woke when they stomped up the stairs and her door thundered open. They dragged her down the steps and pushed her into the kitchen. At first she thought all they wanted was for someone to clean up the mess they had made.

But she was wrong.

As she was pushed from one man to the next Alice began to realize they had something else, something more sinister, in mind.

"Dance for us, Madame."

"Yes, on the table. Give us the can-can."

"*Ja, Frau* Pothron. Dance for us." A soldier, his uniform open at the neck and sweat streaming down his face, screamed with laughter and thumped the table with a fat fist, beer spilling out of his mug and onto the floor.

"Can-can, you little whore, can-can for us."

"Please, ..." Her voice was drowned.

"Please, what?" Another pushed his face forward. A smile like a wolf. It was the corporal, the one she detested the most. He was so close she could smell the beer on his breath and the rancid sweat of his body. He tilted her head up with his finger. "Why no can-can, Madame?"

"Don't touch me."

She pushed his hand away but he grabbed her chin and squeezed. Her panic was lost in the palm of his hand. He gripped a fistful of her hair; bent her head so that his wet lips smeared against her neck.

"Ahh," he muttered taking in the aroma of her clean skin.

He dragged her across the room and pushed her against the table's edge and then with a final heave she was on the table staring up at the circle of men.

"I'm first," he called, pushing the other men aside. "Me first," he screamed again and unbuttoned his trousers.

Don't scream. Don't think. Just let them do it. Don't let Evelyne hear. Let the child sleep. Let her...

don't scream ...

don't let them know ...

don't...

One of the men entered her and thrust. Hard. Through the mist of her humiliation, through the agony that was tearing her body apart she heard someone giggle, then another. The panting men crowded round the table as she lay speared and helpless. They held onto her arms and legs and each waited their turn as one by one they raped her.

She closed her mind to the ordeal. As the pain peaked, she seemed to slide out of her body and for one moment she was above the scene, watching almost dispassionately. It would soon be over. It was not the end of her life. There was always Evelyne. No, she would not scream. She would not give them that satisfaction although every cell in her body yelped and flinched with agony.

She wouldn't...

She wouldn't...

When they were done Alice slipped off the table and on to the floor, lying among the goose feathers and the pools of beer, retching with degradation and pain. Down her legs ran the accumulated stink of the men who had raped her and in her mouth was the salty taste of them.

They left her on the floor; her nightgown torn and her lips bleeding as they staggered away to another house and another party.

Afterwards, she would remember with fearful clarity the buckle on a belt; the eagle resting on a swastika and the words *Gott Mit Uns.* God with us.

CHAPTER 21

> In the midst of winter, I finally learned that
> there was in me an invincible summer.
>
> - Albert Camus

After Germany invaded the USSR on 22 June 1941 many of the soldiers based in France were transferred to the Eastern Front. Paron was slowly emptied of the youngest, fittest and most competent men. They were sent to bolster the over three million German military personnel already in Russia. Among them were the men who had raped Alice. She stood watching as they clambered aboard a troop carrier. They remembered the night of the rape; their smirks and crude hand gestures told her so. They took with them the machinery of war and left behind the sour repugnant memory of violation and the sick awareness that she was pregnant.

For a few days there was an eerie silence in Paron, the residents hoping but without hope that they had seen the last of them. Then in place of the young soldiers came older, slightly corpulent Germans with wispy hair and a more *laissez faire* attitude; their desire was to see the war out in the pleasant comfort of a French home rather than fight a battle. Those assigned to her house made few demands and kept their communication with Alice to a minimum. Her contempt for them and their ilk was obvious and undiminished.

In September 1941, three months after the gang-rape, Alice miscarried. A few days in the Sens hospital where Evelyne had been born were enough for her. In spite of the doctor's advice she went back to Paron, to the house full of German soldiers and to Evelyne who, in her absence, had been taken in by the Jochmans.

The doctors had cared for her as well as they could in a hospital gravely lacking medical equipment and drugs, much of which had been taken by the occupying forces. With each of her previous miscarriages she had lost a little more of her heart, of her body's elasticity and the buoyancy and enthusiasm of her youth. This time hunger and an inner hopelessness had kept her weak and bleeding for too long. What kept her alive, in what was to be her final few months in Paron, was a stubborn almost inflexible determination to see it through for Evelyne's sake.

For once she was pleased she had not gone full-term. It would have been monstrous to have brought a rapist's child into the world and a German one at that. The hurt was more psychological than physical, the disgust with which she remembered the event, that her body had been a toy for those men and her utter helplessness in the face of their predation. It was foul, horrible and she wondered if she would ever forget.

The autumn days slipped slowly past. She continued her daily routines, cooking for the soldiers, washing their clothes that stank of machine oil, sweat and sometimes worse. She prided herself on never letting anyone know the depths of her despair. The only one to whom she could confess, the only one who understood, was Lulu.

By October the days had begun to shorten and the evenings no longer crept warmly in, instead they thundered down upon them in an icy rage. She

190

leaned her head against the wintry glass of a downstairs window watching the first flurries of snow. It was cold outside, most of the leaves lost in an early storm so that the branches stood like a skeleton's reaching out towards her. Winter seemed to have come early to Paron. It always seemed to be winter in Paron. Where had all the summers gone?

It was Tuesday 16 December 1941, a blue-fingered morning, cloudless with a chill that stubbornly hung on the shirt tails of the night. She woke to a heavy mist that softened the countryside like a woolen blanket. It muffled sound so that even birdsong came to her strained, as if through a metal sieve. The church bells of Sens dully clamored the hour through the tendrils of mist that clung to the window. Alice dragged herself out of bed and went downstairs. She lit the stove and prepared breakfast. Everything seemed to take her longer than before, her feet heavy and her fingers clumsy with fatigue. The water pump had become her particular enemy until she had finally assigned one of the soldiers to the chore of bringing in the water.

On that momentous day Lulu arrived breathless at her door.

"Come outside," she said. "Quick, quick."

Alice gathered Evelyne up and joined Lulu on the steps outside.

"What is it?" she asked.

"I've something very important to tell you. I've heard news from the BBC that Germany has declared war on America."

Alice felt a surge of emotion. She was not sure if it was fear or exultation.

"Why? Why now when the worst must surely be over?"

"We may not have seen the worst, not by a long stretch," Lulu said, blowing on her fingers. "Wait until le *boche* has his back to the wall then we'll see what rabid dogs they really are. As for America?" Lulu shrugged. "I expect it has something to do with what happened in Hawaii."

"What happened?"

"Earlier this month Japanese planes bombed Pearl Harbor where your Mr. Roosevelt has his Navy. It was bad. Many killed."

"*Mon Dieu*," Alice whispered. "Now it truly is a world war."

"Anyway, Hitler must be mad to drag America in. Now he is fighting everyone. In the long term he can't hope to win," Lulu said. "But I'm not sure if it will benefit you."

"Why not? The Americans will come over here and sort things out."

"Think, Alice." Lulu said, tapping the side of her head. "Hitler has formally made America the enemy and that means you. You are not merely a foreign alien any longer; you are now an enemy alien."

"Oh, my God. I hadn't thought it through."

"Well, I have," said Lulu looking round, careful that no one heard their conversation.

"They'll put me in a camp. I wouldn't survive. I know it. And what would happen to Evelyne?"

"It gets worse."

"It can't get worse."

There had been a denunciation, Lulu explained. She was not sure who had it in for Alice but it did not bode well for the young American woman. Alice felt sick. There had always been a simmering resentment among some of the women of Paron, she knew that. She was a stranger with strange ways therefore, in their eyes, her morals had to be suspect. Some pointed out that a woman on her own, even the wife of a prisoner-of-war or a widow, and should have no truck with the Germans. It did not seem to matter that they had been billeted on her by the occupying authorities and that she had had no say in the matter. When Lulu left, Alice stood at the kitchen sink wondering how this news would affect her and what she ought to do.

Some days later, Alice heard that *Madame l'épicière* had received the butter allowance. She went early to stand in line, still puzzling over Lulu's news of America's entry into the war and, more immediately, her denunciation. She edged closer to the front of the store and put on her most pleasant expression, hoping *Madame l'épiciére* would oblige with the small pat of butter that was her due.

"No butter for you today, Madame." The woman's voice dripped with satisfaction, a smug look on her face. The look, with its halo of vengeance, told Alice who had denounced her. She ran from the grocery store and down the road with the snow falling around her.

It was this episode that gave her the strength to make a decision. She had to get out of Paron, away from the Germans in her house, away from the suspicions of people like Madame Grocer and find somewhere to hole up and get well again. She was too sick-at-heart, too physically weak and too ill to handle the chores and daily humiliations any longer. Even Louise had, in the past few days, remarked on Alice's frailty and the possibility that she get out of Paron.

The next time she saw Lulu her mind was made up.

"This is sudden."

"Not really." Alice hesitated. She told Lulu of her suspicions about the denunciation. "I'm sure it's her. Not only that," she said. "I'm unwell. I'm fading. I need to get out of here while I still can. I'm afraid if I stay any longer I will die here and then what will happen to Evelyne?"

Lulu nodded slowly. "I agree."

"Emile's auto is still in the garage," Alice said. "I can drive and I'll go to Nice. Can you get me some gas and a new battery?"

"It's not going to be possible," said Lulu. "You need a permit to drive a private vehicle. You would have to go to the authorities and apply and you have no valid reason for permission to be granted. Besides where will you go?"

"To Nice. Emile said ..."

"Darling," Lulu said gently. "Nice is at the other end of the country. Where do you think I'm going to get the gas for this mighty journey across occupied France?"

"There must be a way."

"I'll see what I can do," Lulu said. "Don't worry. We'll get you out of Paron and somewhere safe where you can stay until you're better."

Alice did not stop to wonder at the 'we' in Lulu's statement. Instead, with a rush of affection she stood up, grabbed hold of the prostitute's hand and pulled her to the stairs. She led Lulu to the bedroom she shared with Evelyne. In the cupboard were all the beautiful gowns she had made for her trip on the *Normandie*. They hung in sinuous folds, a rainbow of colors. Alice grabbed them off their hangers; the blue one overlaid with chiffon that looked like fallen sky and the cherry red one with a hem of diamante. The green silk dress she'd worn to their first dinner on board the cruise liner.

"Here," she said, thrusting silk and sequins into Lulu's open arms. "See if they'll fit. If those bastards find them after I've gone they'll only take them back to Germany."

"They're beautiful." Lulu rubbed the material against her cheek. "So sensuous."

"Quick, take them before they come back."

"Now it's my turn to thank you."

Downstairs Alice asked only one question. "*Quand?*" When.

"In a few days," Lulu replied. "Pack a bag and take only what you can carry. You must be ready when I come for you."

After Lulu left, the enormity of her decision began to sink in. She had always been aware that her alien status made her vulnerable. But now that America had entered the war it felt different, more sinister. She remembered the Jewish refugees sitting in the back of the truck, remembered their white faces as they were driven away. If she stayed, she and Evelyne might have to face a journey to nowhere on the back of a truck, just like those poor people.

That night she lay sleepless, while downstairs the soldiers played cards and drank beer. What plans would Lulu make for her? How was she going to manage? Where could she stay until the war was over and she could go back to America?

The problems seemed insurmountable and skittered around her mind like frantic mice. Evelyne would come with her, of course, but she could not take Skippy. Louise would have to look after him. She made a small, silent promise – when it was all over she would come back for him.

And what should she pack? The first things to go into her valise would be the passports, hers and Emile's and Evelyne's birth certificate. Money would go into her underwear. Ration cards and *carte d'identité* in the pocket of her old overcoat. A change of clothes – more for Evelyne. She was barely toilet trained. She would need more than just one change of clothing. Also some bread and cheese. Who knew when they'd eat or where? She should have asked Lulu for more details. But Lulu had been so secretive she probably would not have answered.

That night it snowed again. Heavy flakes drifted calmly down and coated the street and the church and farm opposite. It was so cold, colder than she could remember. She felt it through her thin dress and her skin, now almost transparent and hanging from her bones like old washing, seemed to draw the cold into her heart. Emile would not recognize her now, if he were still alive. No, don't think about it. Think about getting away..

It was hard to pretend that nothing momentous was about to occur. The *boche* still had to be fed, loaves of bread cut, what beetroot jam there was divided between them. There was ersatz coffee that had only its heat to commend it. Emile Jochmans had sent over a few eggs. In a flight of luxury Alice hard-boiled every last one, cut them into halves and set them out for the men, keeping two to add to her luggage.

"Here, wash," one soldier said after breakfast as he shoved at the pile of dirty washing with his foot. "Wash *echt gut.*"

"In a pig's eye," Alice muttered.

The soldiers clattered out, hauling their rifles over the shoulders, leaving a few men to lounge on the floor near the machine guns. Maneuvers again, she thought, a bunch of fat offensive slobs belching and farting and peeing against French walls. Hate bubbled up and she kicked at the dirty washing.

Don't tell me to 'wash good', she grumbled to herself. Wash them yourself, you bastard.

It would be a relief when she left this place. She would never see the kitchen again; never have to scrub that table. She had not eaten off it since the rape. Now she would never have to. Physically she was slowly recovering from the assault, but her mental state was another story. She wanted to believe that terrible half-hour would not color the rest of her life.

She told herself they could sour her future only if she allowed them to. Those thirty minutes were not her life. But it was proving very hard to put the philosophy into practice.

CHAPTER 22

> The courage of the few in some measure redeemed the cowardice of the many.
>
> - Keren M Chiaroni

When the Germans first arrived in 1940 there was little defiance, only a dumb-struck horror. The first resistance occurred when a few ordinary French folk helped the men of the British Expeditionary Force who had been left on the beaches of Dunkirk to escape occupied France. It was as if a few of the ordinary French people understood that if they gave in to oppression they would give up on life itself. And they were not about to do that.

Slowly a resistance of sorts began in Paris, ill-organized and futile. Printing subversive newspapers was not going to achieve anything, except to see the *resistants* shot. But helping escapees, evaders and vulnerable people like Alice was more successful.

In 1940 the Belgian Comet group, headed by the twenty-year-old Dédée de Jongh, had started to assist British escapees and evaders. Her escape line ran from Brussels through Paris to St Jean-de-Luz near the Spanish border and then, with the assistance of Basque guides, over the Pyrenees mountains. The Pat line was run by another Belgian, Dr. Albert-Marie Guérisse (known as Pat O'Leary). Hundreds of members of these escape organizations were captured by the Germans, tortured and either murdered or placed in concentration camps. Only about three percent returned. Both Dédée de Jongh and Pat O'Leary were betrayed and sent to a concentration camp. Fortunately, both survived.

Maisons closes or brothels were sometimes used as 'safe houses' by escape lines. Official registers such as those used in hotels, the official *fiche,* were not used in brothels. As a result, there were no regular inspections, only snap checks by the Germans who were more anxious about the spread of venereal disease than about identifying the patrons.

The house Lulu owned in Sens was a rabbit-warren of passages, stairs and small rooms, some of them used by the 'girls' to conduct their business and others put to a more secretive use.

Lulu had been a 'working girl' for many years. It was her 'profession' and she resented the idea of her workers being considered *filles soumises* or subjected girls who had to be registered and endure regular medical inspections. Lulu hated the constant interference by the *police des mœuers* or vice squad. She had run a brothel before some of them had been born, she told them, which was not quite true but the *gendarmes* who investigated her were generally young, fresh-faced and thoroughly embarrassed.

As poverty and unemployment increased so did the number of women ready to do anything to feed their families, including prostitution. Brothel keepers had an endless supply of young girls and women wanting to enter the 'trade', but Lulu was fussy and only included a few women she thought showed 'the heart of a prostitute'. She had once tried to explain her philosophy to Alice.

"No man wants a woman who is that desperate for her family. What a man wants is someone with an air of elegance, a mystique, as if her mind is on higher things. Think ..." and here Lulu paused. "Think Marlene Dietrich, think Garbo. So *insouciante,* so *formidable.* I can't have shabby desperate women lying there thinking about their hungry children when they are supposed to be looking after the needs of the man."

Alice visited Lulu's brothel only once. On the day of her escape.

It was a few days after their talk about escape that Lulu appeared once more in Alice's kitchen. They walked into the garden where Lulu lit a cigarette.

"There is another person who needs to escape and I think I know a way for you both. We'll need your automobile."

Alice nodded. "You can get the papers? I can drive, you know."

Lulu looked amused. "Yes, you told me about your attempt to escape. It was a rather hit and miss affair, wasn't it, with plenty of hit and not enough miss."

Alice burst into laughter. "Okay, maybe you're right. So, what's the plan?"

Lulu put her hand up and stopped Alice's questions at the source. "No, no questions. In a day or so Monsieur Jochmans will take your auto to the farm and make it ready for use."

"It hasn't been used in over a year. Eighteen months, in fact. Not since *l'exode*," Alice said with relief mixed with apprehension. "So, I'm going to get out at last. Tell me more."

"It's better that you know nothing. We'll all be safer that way," Lulu said, already feeling the sadness of committing her friend to an unknown future. She hesitated. "Alice, are you sure?"

"Yes, of course. I can't stay here any longer. *C'est impossible.* I need to go somewhere where I can get well again. "

Alice began to ready herself for the journey. She took the passports and other documents out of their hiding place and sewed them into the lining of her bag. She kept busy doing last minute mending and packing. Early one morning, before Alice was up, Emile Jochmans took the Citroën out of the garage and pushed it over the road to the farm.

Louise Fromont was fretful about the idea of Alice and Evelyne leaving Paron, although she saw the reason for Alice's need to leave. She had been the one to nurse her in the days following the gang-rape and the miscarriage and, while she did not exactly say it aloud, she thought Alice had been exceptionally stubborn in not reporting the men. Men should not be allowed to get away with something like that. And now Alice was leaving and she might never see her again. She was suddenly overtaken by her affection for the young woman and admiration for her pluckiness.

"Simply walking off like that," she groused. "Where do you think you're going? It's winter. The next we'll hear of you will be two frozen bodies in a ditch."

"But you'll take care of Skippy, won't you? I can't take him with me, *tante.*"

"I should think not." Louise glared at Alice and then softened. "Oh, very well. He can only stay for a little while. You can't expect me to feed a dog when we can hardly feed ourselves."

"*Oui, tante. Merci beaucoup, tante.* Lulu will take him if you can't manage. Or the Jochmans."

"Don't be silly," Louise said huffily. "I'm quite capable of looking after one miserable little dog, thank you."

201

Everything was ready, except for the weather. It had snowed in the night. Large flakes drifted past her window, forming hillocks and small valleys where roads and sidewalks had been. The morning was bright but not with sunlight. It was the sheer brilliance of newly-fallen snow as if it had been lit up from underneath, casting grotesque grey shadows onto itself.

The dishes were washed and she had pumped what she believed was her last bucket of water. There was a freshly ironed pile of shirts on the table. When the soldiers came back later they would find their clothes in order, but would have to cook their own supper. It was over and a new chapter was beginning. Alice felt a surge of excitement.

She sat in the kitchen with Evelyne on her lap. It had to be very, very soon, perhaps today. She could feel a stirring in her bones. Her senses stretched, taking in everything as if to imprint it on her memory; the smell of roasted barley, the sound of voices in the street outside, the stamp of marching feet somewhere in the distance and the barked instructions of an *ausbilder* taking the men through their paces. She thought she could even hear the swastika that flew above the *poste de police* as it flapped and crackled like hooves on cobbles.

So she was not altogether surprised when Lulu appeared at the door and beckoned. Alice picked up the small valise, held Evelyne carefully, the child's sleepy head against her shoulder. She closed the door with a small click. They walked in silence across the bridge to Sens and to the brothel.

As they neared the front door Alice hesitated. "I can't go in there," she said.

Lulu burst out laughing. "At this late stage you're worrying about what people will think? No matter, we're going in by the back door anyway."

Lulu looked around, made sure no one was watching, then turned off the street and led Alice along a short alleyway. It was dark, with uncollected garbage underfoot. Old snow had banked up against the dripping walls. Lulu unlocked a door and pushed Alice through, closing it behind them. The kitchen was warm and inviting with a table set for a meal. Something bubbled fragrantly on the stove and steam rose into the cold morning air. The house was quiet, only the slow ticking of a clock disturbed the silence.

"There's someone I want you to meet," Lulu said, leading Alice to a small room at the back of the house. It was dark, the curtains drawn. Alice could just make out a man lying on the bed, the red circle of a cigarette glowing in the dark. As they entered the figure uncoiled and, in the pale light that filtered through the curtains, Alice saw the silhouette of a tall, thin man. The fractured sunlight spun a coil of bright air around his blond head and sloping shoulders.

Alice shrieked.

A German, dressed in the uniform of the military police, the *Feldgendarmerie* gorget around his neck catching the light.

She had been betrayed.

She turned to run. Lulu roughly grabbed her arm. Alice trembled as Lulu explained that the man, Edward, was a British pilot trying to escape France after his airplane had crashed. They had thought of a way for the two of them to leave together.

Risky? Lulu shrugged at the question. Life in France was a daily risk.

"Pleased to meet you," he said, offering his hand and Alice reluctantly held it for a moment. It was dry and coarse as if he'd been living rough.

"You're English," she said.

He laughed. "Is it so obvious?"

"Only when you open your mouth." She turned to Lulu. "Isn't this dangerous? Don't you know that harboring a British national is *sous peine de mort*? On pain of death?"

"Yes, I know," Lulu said. "I could be shot. And if Edward is caught wearing a German uniform he'll be shot." Lulu gave a wide Gallic shrug. "What can I say? Life under the Nazis is a dangerous affair."

"*Ich spreche Deutsches*," Edward said.

Alice felt cold. A British serviceman who spoke fluent German? Was he for real? What if he were a traitor? Lulu seemed to sense Alice's suspicion.

"Edward wants to return to duty," she explained patiently. "He can do it, Alice. Don't worry."

Edward explained it was important for the war effort that men like him were returned as soon as possible to their home bases. Experienced pilots were priceless and the demand far exceeded the supply. It cost the British government thousands of pounds to train a pilot and the training took weeks.

"We can't afford to lose pilots into POW camps," he said. "I've got to get home."

"Emile Jochmans has the Citroën ready," Lulu said.

"Lulu, are you sure about this?"

Lulu shrugged. "As sure as I can be."

By this time, downed airmen were regularly being passed along sometimes primitive escape lines and the number of successful escapes had become a serious problem for the Germans. On 22 September

1941, General von Stülpnagel issued an edict that any male aiding the crew of enemy aircraft would be immediately shot. Any female helper would be sent to a concentration camp. The escapes continued. It is estimated that over thirty-five thousand Allied soldiers and airmen were returned to England through escape lines such as Lulu's. It is believed that for every Allied man returned to his country one helper died.

At the brothel Lulu explained that Edward, fluent in German and looking very Aryan with his blond hair, blue eyes and soldierly bearing, was going to drive the Citroën out of Paron and through the various road blocks. They would travel south and get as close to the demarcation line as they could. Alice would act the part of his girlfriend with a sick child they were taking to the children's hospital in Lyon.

"If questioned, Edward will have to wing it as we weren't able to get hold of all the required documents."

"We? Who is 'we'?"

"Never mind."

As soon as they were clear of the local road blocks and when Edward thought it wise they would part company and each go their own way. Edward would be in the care of members of another escape line and Alice ...? Lulu sighed. Who knew what to do with this small stubborn American and her baby?

To Alice it sounded like a hare-brained exercise in futility and would surely end tragically. But she had to get out of Paron and if this was the only way then so be it.

"Edward can't take you all the way to Nice," Lulu said as if knowing Alice's thoughts.

"But why not?"

"This masquerade will only work for a short time. Perhaps a day, two days at the most," Lulu said. "After that Edward will be in great danger. Besides, in the free zone a German in uniform would stick out. He just wouldn't be able to carry it off."

"I'm sorry," Alice said. "Of course."

Edward smoothed his hair back and replaced the officer's cap at a jaunty angle. Alice had to admit that he looked German, especially when he clicked his heels and said, "*Tue ich schaue recht?*" Do I look right?

"Perfect," Lulu said smiling. She turned to Alice. "You have to play your part. You can do this?"

Alice nodded. It seemed crazy, to say the least. But if Lulu thought it could work then she would go along with it. Life in a house full of German soldiers was no longer an option. She was too sick, too emotionally lost to handle it any longer. Somewhere in Nice she would hole up and get well again, wait for all this to end and then find her way back to America.

They walked out of the brothel, back across the bridge and down the hill to the Jochmans farm. Behind them marched Edward, his cane tucked importantly under his arm. Alice noticed the deference with which the guard on the bridge saluted him and had to admit he played the part of a German officer to perfection.

At the farm Godelieve showered kisses on Evelyne's cheeks and hugged Alice. She pressed a parcel of food into her hands and M. Jochmans cranked the car. It caught immediately. He patted the bonnet and gave Edward a thumbs-up.

They climbed into the Citroën, Edward in the driver's seat and Alice in the back with a very subdued Evelyne on her lap.

As Edward drove carefully out of the farm gate Lulu waved, her eyes brimming with tears.

"Godspeed," she whispered. "*Vive la France, vive l' Amérique.*"

CHAPTER 23

> Life's but a walking shadow, a poor player
> That struts and frets his hour upon the stage
> And then is heard no more.
>
>   - William Shakespeare

At first it all seemed to go well. Edward stopped at the first road block and shouted at the guards. The bombast in his voice carried them through, especially when Alice upped the drama by crying loudly. Evelyne added a touch of realism with her infuriated bawling whenever Alice pinched her lightly on her bottom.

They got through the next two road blocks without trouble. The guards at the barricades showed little interest in a German officer and his rather hysterical girlfriend. After each barricade she felt a little more confident, a little less fearful. The guards barely looked at the occupants of the auto, merely raised the wooden barricade and allowed Edward to drive through. But the further they got from Paron and the closer to big towns, the more difficult it became. The guards appeared more suspicious and Edward had to argue longer and become more strident, banging the driver's side door to emphasize whatever point he was making.

And then it happened. Beyond a particularly suspicious road block the Citroën gave a slight lurch to one side and the steering wheel dragged in Edward's hands. He cursed and brought the automobile to a stop.

"What is it? What's happened?" asked Alice.

"I think we've got a flat tire." Edward got out and walked around the vehicle. "Yes, I'm afraid so," he said, poking his head in through the window. "This is a rum do. We'll have to wait for a convoy and then flag them down. Then we'll have to trick our way through."

"Can't you fix it?"

Edward shook his head. "It wouldn't do for a German officer to be seen changing a tire."

Fear settled like a cold stone in the pit of Alice's stomach and she began to cry. This time the tears were real.

"*Mon Dieu*," she whispered over the head of her sleeping child.

They did not have long to wait. Within the hour they heard the familiar rumble of heavy vehicles coming towards them. Alice shivered. It would not take any acting on her part to play the distressed girlfriend. A convoy of several trucks slowed and then stopped. The driver leaned out of the cab and shouted.

"*Was ist das problem, Kapitane?*"

"*Wie sie sehen,*" replied Edward, pointing to the flat tire.

There was a discussion between the driver and several of the soldiers. Two jumped off the back of the lead truck and hastened over, their Mauser Karabiner rifles clanking at their sides.

This is the end, Alice thought. Now I'll have to watch Edward being shot at the side of the road and we will be taken to a camp. But instead, Alice was courteously asked to step out of the automobile. A young soldier whipped off his overcoat and spread it on the cold ground where he invited Alice, with Evelyne sleeping like a bundle of washing in her arms, to sit while they repaired the tire. Edward casually accepted a cigarette from the driver as the men quickly jacked up the Citroën and changed the wheel. There was banter and a few snide looks at Alice. Edward laughed and shrugged.

Looking back Alice thought she'd sat on the German's overcoat for hours but, in reality, it was probably only about ten minutes. All the while the Germans talked, throwing her small glances and wide grins. She knew they were talking about her and her 'relationship' with this German officer. Nasty minded little brutes, she thought.

As they finally drove away, after casual thanks and a swift handshake from Edward, she leaned over to the front seat.

"And just what were they saying?"

"Compliments, Mrs. Pothron. The consensus was that I was a pretty lucky fellow."

"How far are we going?"

"As far as a tank of petrol will allow," Edward said. "And after that ..."

Alice tried to calculate how far a tank of gas would take them, but it was impossible. Towards late afternoon they drove through Avrolles, skirted St Florentin and crossed the bridge over the river Armançon. Traffic was light but there had been another moment of terror when a convoy of light military vehicles passed them going north. Edward waved at them as they swept past. It was a gesture of superb impertinence.

"Oh, heavens," was all Alice could manage.

Later she tried to find out where they were going. To Noyers-sur-Serein, he said.

"And tomorrow?"

Edward shrugged.

"You must know," Alice prompted.

"No, I don't," he said, his voice sharp. "I'm taking it as it comes, from day to day. It's the only way."

"It would help if you remembered to drive on the right side of the road," she said.

"Sorry." Edward swerved.

For the most part he drove silently. Give him his due, she thought. He had been impersonating an enemy officer all day, speaking to them, joking with them. He must be exhausted. But so was she. She thought instead about Lulu and wondered how she had managed to get a German uniform with all its accoutrements. Did some poor Nazi leave the brothel in his underwear? The silly thought pleased her.

She felt grateful for the help given to her, not only by Lulu but by M. Jochmans. And, of course, by this tall young man from England. It had all gone so smoothly and it suddenly occurred to Alice that Lulu must have done this before. The organization that had gone into this escape was not off-the-cuff. It had the feel of a well-turned machine. She felt a profound new respect for her friend, the glamorous prostitute.

As evening stole over the fields, a haunted mist clung to the branches of trees that lined the road and lifted like wraiths from the ditches. A few people along the verges of the road were walking shadows that faded into the mist as soon as they passed.

They finally came to the outskirts of the medieval town of Noyers-sur-Serein. They spotted a young boy sitting on a stone wall, a small gargoyle in gabardine. He waved at them, jumped down and disappeared. Edward turned the auto between the tall gateposts of a farmyard and stopped. Behind him the gates clanged shut. The enclosure was walled with ancient rocks etched by moss and lichen. Square bales of hay filled a large shed and light from the open farmhouse door carved a yellow pathway across the cobbled courtyard. Three men ran up, opened the doors and pulled Edward and Alice out.

"*Vite, vite,*" they whispered. Quick, quick. "*Dépêchez-vous ...*" Hurry up.

Someone took a sleeping Evelyne from Alice's arms and carried her through the door into the warm kitchen. Alice clutched her small valise, her feet so cold she stumbled across the doorstep. Evelyne lay on a low couch covered by a crochet blanket. She turned over, making a small mewling noise like a satisfied cat and settled back to sleep.

Standing by the table was a young woman, her hair in a long dark braid. She glanced up, her face guarded, and went on cutting bread. Several large earthenware plates stacked with food stood ready. Alice went to her, hand outstretched.

"*Je m'appelle ...*"

"No names," the woman said smiling, holding up a farm-roughened hand. "Better that way."

They sat and ate quickly and in silence, Edward still in his purloined uniform. The three men had cleared their plates, gone outside and when the young woman took Alice and Evelyne out to the courtyard, they were nowhere to be seen. Neither was the automobile.

"But, where's the car?" Alice asked. "I thought we were going on."

The woman gestured towards the bales of hay. "It makes a good hiding place, no?"

"And Edward?"

"He will stay here tonight. Someone is coming for you in a few minutes and will take you and your child into Noyers town."

"Will I see Edward in the morning?"

"No, Madame. He must go another way."

"Then I must thank him. What he did was brave beyond duty."

"Quickly then."

Alice re-entered the kitchen. Edward sat at the table with his back to her. She slipped her arms around his shoulders, feeling the scrape of epaulettes, and laid her cheek alongside his.

"Thank you, dear man, and God speed."

He squeezed her hands and she slipped out of the warm kitchen without ever seeing his face again.

"Now to Noyers," the woman said as Alice rejoined her. "You will be safe there, at least for tonight."

"And tomorrow?"

The woman was saved from answering by a man riding a bicycle through the opened gateway and towing another next to him.

"*Bonsoir,*" the man called. "Quickly now, we must be inside before curfew."

The woman with the braided hair, that was how Alice would remember her, placed a foggy-brained Evelyne into the carrier basket of the second bicycle while the man grabbed Alice's bag and began pedaling away.

With a certain amount of apprehension, Alice mounted the bicycle. She had not ridden one for many years. She wobbled into the dark street with Evelyne nervously clutching the edges of the basket. Finally she found her balance and sped to catch up with the man in front. Soon the farmhouse was behind them, drifting away into the snow. They rode in silence through a medieval gateway and into Noyers. The man gestured for Alice to ride down a small road while he went straight ahead and disappeared into the dark. A few yards, a few closed doors and a man stepped out of the shadows.

"*Bonsoir*, Madame," he said grabbing hold of the handlebars. "You've arrived. Your luggage came a moment ago so we knew you were here."

Alice had learned not to ask questions, merely to be thankful for the many people prepared to help. She could not imagine the danger in which such ventures put them and their families. Edward had been silent when she'd asked about the German *Feldgendarmerie* uniform. All he had said was, "Such questions could have Lulu up against a wall with a bullet in her brain." Alice remembered subsiding into the leather back seat, appalled at the risk strangers had taken for her and the organization that must have gone into her escape. She began to accept there were braver, kinder people in the world than she had ever imagined.

There had been a frosty reception from the outset when the arrogant and imperious Germans had marched into their country, although the conquerors had behaved, initially, with civility. Hitler had insisted there would be no uncontrolled violence against the French. But it was not long before the Nazis showed their true colors, and began a systematic reign of terror. French citizens were suddenly faced with moral choices they had never even thought of before. Shamefully, some of the French chose to collaborate with the enemy, some more eagerly than others. Some became so enmeshed in the evil of occupation that they betrayed their friends and colleagues, who were arrested, tortured and put to death. Most did only what they had to do in order to survive.

A small core of Frenchmen chose defiance and resistance in the face of increasingly brutal repression. These people formed the basis of what was to become the Resistance as well as the heroic escape lines. And now, thanks to Lulu and her unknown friends, she and Evelyne were the fortunate recipients of a full-scale assisted escape.

The man took the bicycle from her, carried it up the stairs and wheeled it into the house. She followed him into the kitchen. Her bones ached, her throat felt raw and her heart beat so loudly she wondered if it could be heard all the way to Paron. By now the men in her house would be aware she was gone. Would there be a full-scale search for her? Was she already on some 'most wanted' list? Probably not, but the thought still chilled her to the bone.

A fire in the large brick fireplace drew Alice's attention and she moved towards it, her hands outstretched. Above it hung a row of copper pots gleaming dully. A small intense woman stood at the kitchen sink. She came forward and smiled as she bent down to kiss Evelyne's cold cheek.

"I am Isabelle," she said. "And you have met my husband, Jean-Louis. It's better if you go to the bedroom. If someone looks through the window and sees a stranger there will be questions."

Alice stumbled after the woman, up a short flight of stairs to a bedroom with a sloping ceiling. A hot water bottle had been placed between the sheets, Isabelle said, and the bed looked inviting.

"*Bonne nuit,*" Isabelle whispered, leaving a candle on the bedside table.

Alice managed to get Evelyne's coat and shoes off before they tumbled onto the bed. She closed her eyes and blanked out the snowy world full of sorrows, shadows and whispers.

It felt as if she had just fallen asleep when she heard loud voices and clattering footsteps in the street below.

She went to the bedroom door, opened it a crack, saw Isabelle with her finger to her lips.

"Shh. *Soyez très tranquille.*" Be very still.

They waited for loud hammering on the door, signaling an inspection, a search, a quick arrest. Waited for a voice to shout, '*ouvrez, s'il vous plait*'. Open.

But it was the house next to Isabelle's. The front door smashed open. There was shouting. Then silence. The soldiers were out in the street again. This time a man hung between them.

Then they were gone.

CHAPTER 24

You may chain my hands and shackle my feet;
you may even throw me into a dark prison,
but you shall not enslave my thinking
because it is free.

- Kahlil Gibran

Sunlight bounced off morning snow and filled the air with blinding diamonds of light. Alice and Evelyne sat in the kitchen eating bread smeared with *confiture,* a jam made from grape skins. Isabelle told Alice that she and Jean-Louis made their own wine and the *confiture* was made in her kitchen.

"Once the juice has been extracted the grape skins are mixed with grapo sweetener and the end result is an almost acceptable jam," said Isabelle proudly.

The coffee was once again roasted barley, chicory and ground acorns, but it did not matter. Last night Alice had slept well and life was good. She wondered who it was who had not been so lucky.

"What had he done?"

Isabelle shrugged. "They don't need an excuse. We have collaborators all around us and no one is safe. He might have been denounced by someone with a grudge."

Alice remembered her own denunciation and shuddered.

She thought of her journey south with Edward and wondered what had happened to the Citroën. Perhaps she could still use it to get to Nice. She had held onto the ridiculous notion that Edward, in his smart German uniform, was going to drive her all the way to Nice on the Mediterranean, a distance of about two hundred and fifty miles. Now, with the morning as bright as shards of glass, she realized how stupid that thought had been. But how was she going to get from Noyers to Nice? When Alice questioned Isabelle, she was under no illusions.

"You walk." The tone was that of a kindly teacher speaking to a rather slow pupil.

"Walk? In winter? With a baby?"

Isabelle shrugged. "It can be done."

"My auto?"

Isabelle did not reply.

"So, no Edward and no automobile. What about the trains?"

Isabelle shrugged again. "If you have the right documents."

Alice tried to imagine Edward bereft of his German uniform. He was too tall and too blond to fit into a French crowd. French men were shorter and the women could be called *petite*. A generalization, she realized, but Edward just did not look Continental. He looked like what he was - very Eton, very English. How was he going to get away, she wondered? More to the point, how was she going to get away?

Without Edward and with no means of transport, the Nice idea was beginning to look more and more ridiculous. Yet Emile had said she must go to Nice and he could be waiting there for her. If he were still alive, she thought. Was that even possible? For a bleak moment she felt truly alone. Then she thought of Henri.

"I need to go to Besançon," she said impetuously.

Isabella looked startled. "Besançon? But why?"

She did not have to be alone in her flight from France, if that was what she was doing. There was Henri, her brother. She knew Noyers was not too far from Besançon. There must be a train or a bus and she remembered the bar where he worked. She needed Henri. Now that Emile was dead, her brother was the only relative she cared about. Except, of course, for Evelyne.

She told Isabelle the story of the orphanage, of how she had found her brother after all those years, working in a bar on the seedier side of town. She tried to find words to explain how important it was for her to find him.

"If he wants to get out of France perhaps we can do it together," she said. "If not, then I might be able to stay with him. In any event, I must get to Besançon to see him."

Isabelle shook her head. Too dangerous, she said. You don't have the right papers. In Besançon there was a prison for foreign alien women. The Caserne Vauban, an old military barracks turned to a bitter use.

"You and the child...," she said, hesitating.

"Nevertheless..."

"You're a stranger," Isabelle said. "You will be noticed."

A stubborn look passed over Alice's face. Still Isabelle tried to dissuade her. Many French reported on strangers, Jews in hiding, odd characters who did not seem to fit in, people who loitered. They got a reward from the Germans. It was unthinkable to put herself and her child in such danger, Isabelle said, desperate to the last. A city was a dangerous place.

"I understand, but small villages aren't much better. I lived in Paron for many months, until someone denounced me."

Isabelle looked shocked. "I suppose that was why you had to get out."

"It was one reason. Now, tell me about Besançon."

Isabelle threw her hands up in a gesture of despair. "You are a stubborn woman," she said, smiling. "Alright, you can't go to Besançon by train as you don't have papers. Go by bus. It's safer because the inspectors don't always look at documents on the buses."

Next morning, Alice caught the early bus to Besançon. Standing room only, she was pressed in on all sides and unable to change Evelyne from one arm to the other. Her arms ached and her shoulders burned with strain. They rumbled and jerked along and Alice could understand why documents were not inspected. There was no room to move.

They passed over one of the seven bridges spanning the Doub River and into the city center. As Isabelle had warned, it was crowded and every second person seemed to be in the drab *feld-grau* uniform of the invaders. Each had a rifle slung over his shoulder and looked quite capable of using it.

At the bus station she found the nearest public telephone kiosk. On the back cover of the phone book was a local map. She carefully plotted her walk along back streets where there would, hopefully, be fewer soldiers. Alice hefted Evelyne onto a hip and began to walk.

It felt like a century ago when she and Emile had visited Besançon in their shiny new Citroën. They had been so carefree, so much in love, not knowing that their days together were numbered. Long, lazy days had stretched out before them, filled with sunlight and music and good food. Perhaps she had seen it through blinkered eyes, having Emile at her side and an unknown baby swimming like a tadpole in her womb.

When she found the bar, it seemed more squalid than she remembered, its sawdust-covered floor scuffed and the counter stained with spilled wine. Conversation and a board game stopped as she walked in. She knew it was not considered correct for a woman to enter a bar, especially with a child, but these were exceptional times, calling for a different code of behavior.

"Henri Guyonvernier?" She whispered to the barman. "Is he here?"

The man shook his head. Henri had left, the man said. Heard he was working in Arbois down the road.

"Arbois? Is it far?"

"No. There's a bus."

"Do you know where he's working?"

"Café Rosa, I think, near the bus stop." He brushed her aside as an elderly man came forward holding his wine glass up for a refill.

She stood outside, still buoyed by the thought of seeing Henri again. She was only dimly aware that a man had followed her out of the bar and was now standing discreetly at her elbow.

"I heard you were looking for Henri," he said. "You are a wife or girlfriend?"

"*Sœur.*"

"Ah, his sister." He nodded. "He spoke of you. Said you were *l'Americain.* Are you going to Arbois to find him?"

She said nothing so he went on. "Just thought you might like to know the bus station is heavily patrolled."

"I know. I've just come from there."

He looked startled. The soldiers were stopping everyone, he said, searching bags and checking documents. Today they had seemed particularly intent, looking for someone special perhaps? The man looked at her with raised eyebrows. Alice wondered if the hunt was on for Edward. She hoped it was not for her, but she remembered Isabelle's information about Caserne Vauban, the prison in Besançon for foreign aliens. Had she almost walked into a *rafle?* She knew about these raids. Lulu had told her.

The man was still speaking, a cigarette stuck to his lower lip. He suggested the river; someone he knew could get her downriver by boat where there was an out-of-town bus stop. Safer, he said. No checks. He did not say any more, just started walking. She followed him, Evelyne on her hip and the valise banging against her thigh.

She wondered if she was safe with this stranger, going past silent buildings to the river bank. Would it be better to risk the busy town center? It was only when they got to a small stone quay; moss covered and slippery, that she learned he was a friend of Henri's. The man told her they had lived in a small boarding house near the bar and both had worked the nightshift.

"Wait here," the man said. "I'll arrange for someone to come. Say *bonjour* to Henri for me."

Alice sat down on a stone bench with Evelyne on her lap and closed her eyes. When she looked up the man was gone. It was only then she realized he had not given her his name. Never mind, Henri would know.

She was tired, so tired, confused by the strange faces and helping hands, tired beyond anything she had ever felt. Her head spun so that events became blurred. She tried to sort out the sequence of things. First, there was Lulu and Edward. Then there were the people at the farmhouse outside Noyers who had hidden the Citroën. After that, it was Isabelle. She thought of the Germans who came for the man next door, but who might have been looking for Edward. Now, this young man. She wondered how many images there would be before it was over and she and Evelyne were safe.

The sun reluctantly peeped through racing snow-packed clouds. An hour, then two, and they were still alone. The river was wide and busy. She watched as grey painted barges glided by and small rowing boats jerked along in their wake.

A Skoda automobile drove along the narrow road behind her. She froze, knowing the Gestapo favored these Czech-made vehicles. It slowed; the occupants stared at her and then drove on, the Nazi insignia flapping from the mudguard. Alice found herself trembling. By early evening she had all but given up and was about to walk away and find a place to sleep when a reed-thin voice called to her. At first she could not place where the voice was coming from.

"Down here," he said.

Tucked into the river's edge, a small fishing boat hung in the water. An old man sat athwart the seat, oars on the gunwale. He beckoned to her. This must be her next contact. She carefully walked down the stone steps holding Evelyne's hand. They clambered into the boat and settled on the seat facing the old man.

"I've waited all day for you," she said, weary beyond politeness.

The man shrugged. He slowly began to move the boat along the river, pulling at the oars and a wake rippled behind them. He explained, they would go down river and he would drop her off near the bus stop. If accosted, she was his granddaughter and they were fishing for their supper. Alice nodded.

She explained her desire to get to Nice. Was there some way she could get across the demarcation line? He shrugged again. It was not his problem. All he had been told was to take the woman and her child down river. He rowed steadily, passing under one bridge and then another. Alice caught sight of vivid patterns of algae striping the ancient stones as they passed beneath bridges that trembled with heavy traffic that raced overhead.

Suddenly the old man stiffened, stopped rowing and sat still. He held up a hand, gesturing to her to be quiet. In the distance Alice heard a faint sound, a chugging noise that rumbled and coughed towards them. To Alice it was indistinguishable from the other motorized sounds on the river – but the old man knew.

Quickly he threw out a fishing line. Through the evening mist rising from the river they saw the sleek grey lines of a boat approaching them. It throttled back.

"*Actung!* What are you doing here?"

"Fishing for our supper," he called. "Is it permitted?"

"*Jawohl*, but it's time you went home. You break curfew, we shoot." The German laughed as the boat drifted closer. "Here," he called. There was something in his hand. He threw it and it landed in the bottom of the boat. For one dreadful moment Alice thought he had thrown a grenade.

"*Danke*," the old man smiled up at him, a fake smile but one that was expected.

The German boat accelerated and roared away, foaming wake catching the small boat and rocking it gently. The old man cleared his throat and spat into the water.

"Bastards!"

Alice hung on to Evelyne, the other hand on the side of the boat. She looked down at the small bar of chocolate the German had thrown into the boat. She grabbed it, resisting the desire to throw it back.

"Damn him," she snarled. "He thinks he can buy us so cheaply."

"Never mind. We'll soon send them scuttling back to their rat's holes with their tails between their legs."

While Alice was still working out the mismatched image he broke off a piece of chocolate and gave it to Evelyne.

"Make sure she has a good life," he said, looking at Alice from under his wild grey eyebrows.

CHAPTER 25

War does not determine who is right -
only who is left.

- Bertrand Russell

Alice boarded the bus to Arbois just beyond the river Doub. It was getting late and beginning to feel like a wild-goose chase, trying to find a brother who might not want to be found. Again, there was standing room only as the bus jolted its slow way south. She was vaguely aware of mutterings around her as men sat defiantly on the slatted wooden benches while women had to stand. They made sure the men knew they were the mothers of France and should be treated accordingly. Alice was happy just to be on the bus, even if she also had to stand holding a weary Evelyne in her arms.

As the barman had said, the Café Rosa was not far from the bus stop. But once again, Alice was out of luck.

"He's not here. Moved on a month ago. Don't know where he went."

Mysteries and secrets. Standing in the Café Rosa opposite a man who perhaps knew but would not tell, she was plunged into a depth of despair such as she had seldom felt. She had been banking on finding Henri, having someone to share the burden and loneliness of escape. Now she was finally, and irrevocably, on her own.

"If you know where he is, just tell him his sister Alice was here."

He nodded and she turned to leave.

"Wait," he said. "Where are you going?"

"To Nice, if I can get there."

He must have taken pity on Alice for he explained that Arbois was just on the border between occupied France and the so-called 'free' zone or Vichy France. He knew a man, a guide, who could take her, who knew when the Germans and their dogs patrolled, knew the easiest route to follow. One hundred and fifty francs. Not expensive for what you got – a safe path to freedom.

It was that easy. One hundred and fifty francs, a shy young man with long greasy hair, a short path through the snowy woods and she was in Vichy France. In Alice's mind, crossing the border between the occupied and the free zones had assumed major proportions. She imagined German guards with machine guns at concrete barricades. At best, she imagined being turned back, at worst being loaded onto a truck and taken away. Yet, in the end, all it took was a young man and a few francs.

It was already dark as she began to walk south, drawn as if by a magnet towards Nice. As the night set in, her footsteps slowed. She began to count, concentrating hard on each step, her feet wet and cold. A sleeping Evelyne felt heavier than ever. Twice, she was passed by transporters filled with French *gendarmes,* but she went on walking, merely moving onto the verge, too shaky to jump into a ditch in case she did not have the strength to get out again.

She walked until she could walk no longer, and still she continued walking as icy flakes slid down her cheeks. Reality soon blended into the mute brilliance of snow. The world closed in, until it was only herself and the baby, the gaunt arms of shrouded trees above her and the icy snow that crunched underfoot.

The road lay like a dark wet carpet stretching into infinity. Evelyne was as heavy as a badly packed suitcase, all limp arms and shoes knocking against Alice's thighs. She walked on through the night, her feet on automatic drive until daylight flushed the surrounding snow with pink. The morning was crisp and clear. She was no longer even sure she was walking south. Perhaps she had been going in circles. She wondered how far she could walk before she finally stopped.

Out of the blind dawn a cart filled with hay stopped beside her. A young farmer gallantly wiped snow off the seat. She was too weak to clamber up on her own so he lifted her and Evelyne up. They moved along a small country lane bordered by a canal until they came to a farmhouse. Along the fence the branches of trees rustled, naked in the air. The smell of manure greeted them, a clean aroma and one Alice would forever associate with the stoic kindness of the rural French people. The farmhouse was low-built. Out of the chimney rose a thin spiral of smoke.

Later, in the warm kitchen, Alice explained her need to get to Nice.

"It's a long way, Madame."

She nodded.

"Look outside and tell me if you think it is traveling weather." He pointed to the thick snow and the watery sun.

When Alice was silent he went on, a shy smile creasing his face.

"Of course, you have walked through it. But, you are through the worst, Madame. You and your child are over the demarcation line. Someone help you over?"

Alice nodded.

He went on. "Around here the border is well-guarded but not with any regularity, not since customs officers replaced the soldiers in February. You come from Arbois?"

"Yes," Alice said.

The farmer's wife placed a bowl of something hot in front of her and she began to eat, lifting the spoon to her lips, hardly aware of the motion. The food and the kitchen fire soothed her, so that all she wanted was to join Evelyne asleep on the horsehair sofa.

She's so good, Alice thought, watching her child. She never complains. She walks when she can and doesn't cry when she can't. Alice thought her baby had every reason to cry. It felt as if they had been eternally cold and wet, always hungry and always feeling lost in the vast countryside of France.

After she and Evelyne had eaten, the wife insisted on showing her to a small bedroom with a window that looked out on the farmyard and the road beyond. Never before had a bed looked so welcome. They lay down, mother and child, and slept.

Later, when the snow storm had abated somewhat, the farmer took her along a narrow road, his snow-clad sheep grazing on either side. They reached a gate in the fence.

"Now remember, Madame, on the occupied side it is one hour ahead of us here the south. If you have a watch it's time to adjust it now. And be careful, Madame, the gendarmes are not the Gestapo but they are sometimes not far behind," he said. "You never know. Some of them will turn a blind eye and some will haul you in. You just don't know which ones to trust."

"You speak from experience?"

The farmer nodded. "The people too. You never know who is a collaborator and who you can trust. It's best not to trust anyone."

After leaving the farmer, with deep gratitude, she did a lot more walking. Sometimes she carried Evelyne and sometimes, through sheer exhaustion, she allowed the child to stomp along beside her. When darkness fell they lay under the trees, Evelyne wrapped in her mother's arms. They woke with frost crackling on their coats. The days and nights began to blur. Alice thought they got a lift in a cart and they were taken to a house where she fell into a nervous half-sleep, always fearful and always on the alert. She remembered the young farmer's advice and constantly worried that someone would turn them in.

Most of the help they got was from taciturn, wretchedly poor rural folk, living a subsistence life with only enough to feed themselves, but always finding a bit more to give to her and Evelyne. They were quietly generous with what little they had. They did not know her name and she did not offer any information except to say that she needed to get to Nice.

On the third, or perhaps the fourth day of walking, she accepted a lift with a silent man driving a small cart laden with hay. As they pulled up behind the farmhouse there was a rustling in the straw behind her and a tall man jumped out and ran into a shed.

"You didn't see that, Madame."

Alice found the energy to smile. "No, I didn't."

Another grey farmhouse deep in the hills, this time no chickens but a large pig that grunted in front of the fireplace in the kitchen.

"Toilet?" Alice asked the woman who came to the door.

"No toilet. Use the trees," the woman said, pointing. "Not behind the hen house, that's where I go and not behind those trees over there. That's my daughter's place."

Alice was getting used to squatting behind trees. The air grew warmer as she travelled south along the endless roads that led towards the Mediterranean. But in spite of the soft comfort of the more temperate days she could feel her strength ebbing. Evelyne grew heavier with each passing day. Alice lost her breath and her arms felt weaker even before the feeble sun was at its height. A nagging pain in her chest signaled that something was seriously wrong. This was not just the weakness of a woman who had suffered a miscarriage only months before and who had, for the past eighteen months been on a near starvation diet. Nor was it the weakness of a woman who was walking the length of France with a baby in her arms. She was only in her mid-thirties. Surely she should be stronger than this? Something was seriously wrong.

When she felt she was at her lowest, a young man stopped to give her a lift. He drove an odd-looking automobile with the sign *plombier* painted on the side, although there were no plumbing tools that she could see. She placed Evelyne on the seat between them and gratefully got in. The young man changed gears and chugged away, black smoke billowing in their wake.

Alice had enough energy to be surprised at the vehicle. Gas had long been unavailable, except for the Germans and on the *marché noir*. Black market prices were extortionate and had been so from the beginning. Some people had used their initiative and turned their cars into either wood burning or coal-fired vehicles. She later heard some autos were run on manure from the farm, but that sounded too preposterous. The plumber's van was one of these innovations; a *gazogène* fuelled by charcoal.

The young man explained. There was a cylinder, installed under the fender, which was filled and ignited. After a few minutes, methane gas was fed through a filter into a special mixing system. The use of solid fuel reduced the horsepower by about twenty percent, he said, but it meant that he had transport, other than a bicycle, cart or his feet. Tires were a problem and usually had to be bought on the black market but, he reasoned, if you could afford to drive a car then you could probably afford to buy tires.

Their route was not along any main road, but instead on a rutted byway, through a dark silent forest and over a stone bridge.

"Where are we going?" shouted Alice above the screech of the wind and the cheeky chatter of the automobile engine. "Where are you taking me?"

"To my grandmother's house," he yelled.

Alice had woken that morning with a feeling of tightness in her chest. For days her sinuses had been aching and she had developed a deep dry unsatisfying cough. She knew the symptoms; a bad cold or even a bout of bronchitis. She felt desperately cold and shivery. Her resolve and energy had been worn down to a nub. It had not helped that her paper thin shoes had been wet since she had left Paron.

Finally, they crested a hill in a blaze of noise and black smoke and she saw far below a toy farm set out beneath them, a Lilliputian collection of grey stone buildings. There were two tall cypresses, one on each side of the gate. One for *la paix* and one for *la prospérité*, he explained, traditional. Peace and prosperity – a far-off dream.

Alongside the short winding dirt road to the front door were rows of vines, dry and brown against the snow. The young man drove the *gazogène* round the back of the house and into an open shed.

Evelyne was awake and crying. "It's all right," Alice said, planting a cold kiss on her forehead.

An old woman stood at the back door. She was dressed in the customary way of respectable rural women, only the patched areas still a bombazine black. Her wrinkled hands held on to a gnarled walking stick. Alice's mind turned to Besançon and her childhood in the orphanage. She remembered such women coming down to the river to wash clothes. They would cluck sympathetically at her busy little hands. The memory was fuzzy and rebounded in her aching head.

The old woman made no move to help Alice as she struggled up the stone stairs, Evelyne slack on her shoulder and her feet clumping in time to the dull thud of pain in her head.

"*Bonjour, grand-mère,*" the young man called. "*J'ai un colis pour vous.*" I have a parcel for you.

"We call all our visitors 'parcels'," he said apologetically to Alice. "It's not meant impolitely or frivolously. It's just that we need to distance ourselves from the people we help. It would not pay to get emotionally involved, you see."

"And I don't want to know too much either," she mumbled through cold-stiffened lips.

The kitchen was warm with a fire glowing at one end. Overhead, pots and pans hung from hand-chiseled wooden beams. A few stray hens clucked across the red tiled floor and scrabbled for a footing as the old woman shooed them out of the way.

To one side, a wind-up gramophone stood on spindly legs. It was similar to one she and Emile had at home in San Francisco and to which they had jitterbugged in youthful abandon. A handle on the side wound it up. There were needles that had to be changed every time a record was played. They had not been available since the war started. And besides, Vichy was not keen on people playing music, and dancing was forbidden. It went against the Vichy demand for sacrifice, that no one should enjoy themselves while they were 'in mourning' after the defeat. The people in this farmhouse had taken Pétain's restrictions to heart, for across the gramophone was draped a wide black sash.

A yellow cloth on the table brightened the room, but Alice noticed its circumference had begun to whirl unaccountably.

How odd, she thought as she put Evelyne down and grabbed the edge of the table.

"I am not well, Madame," she managed to say before she sat heavily in the nearest chair.

CHAPTER 26

A journey is best measured in friends
rather than miles.

- Tim Cahill

Alice woke slowly. She was lying in a double bed,
clothed in a large scratchy woolen shirt. She could
not remember how she got there or when.
A shaft of sunlight slipped through the half-open
curtains and pooled on a small rug on the floor. On
the wall a gaudy painting of fishing boats drifted
against an idyllic and impossibly blue sea. The floral
wallpaper danced before her eyes. To the side was a
large bloated wardrobe, all curlicue and walnut. It
was a typical *petit-bourgeois* bedroom. She wondered
whose it was, but felt too weak to explore the matter
further.
How long had she been asleep? Her throat felt
scratchy and her head ached. Around her neck was a
poultice of some sort, its pungent aroma filling her
nostrils. She sat up slowly. A pink satin eiderdown
slithered to the floor as an old woman floated into
her vision.
"Are you hungry?"
"Yes, *grand-mère.*"
The old woman left the room and returned with
a plate of soup and a piece of bread on a tray.
Following directly on her heels was Evelyne.
"Now, don't worry your *Maman*. Let her eat and
then rest again." Evelyne was quickly ushered out of

the room. The old woman turned back. "Is there anything more I can do for you, Madame?"

"*Non, merci.* You have been very kind."

"You need a doctor."

"No. No doctor," she croaked. "I am better, *grand-mère,* much better."

Alice was afraid to move her head in case it fell off her shoulders. It was still ached and fuzzed and she could hear sea sounds in her ears. It felt as if she had wandered through a nightmare. In a dull sort of reprise, as if she needed to repeat the names so that they would remain forever in her mind, she remembered Edward and the Noyers lady. What was her name? Isabelle. A bicycle and the bruised ache of her bones. Besançon where she had looked for Henri. The *gazogène* and a young man. She still had a long way to go before she got to Nice and Emile.

But he was dead. She fell back on the pillows with a dry sob.

A day later and she was well enough to sit with the two old women in the kitchen that smelled of feathers and the stale odor of unopened windows. Farmhouse meals usually consisted of soup, bread, honey and pork pâté. This farmhouse was no different and there was wine for the adults and milk for Evelyne.

"Where is your grandson? I would like to thank him."

Neither woman answered and Alice realized she was again in the middle of a family with secrets.

"Do you think he could get me papers to travel on the train?"

Again, there was no answer. She wondered if the young man was in one of the *degaullist* movements. There were rumors of budding dissident groups in the south who were disillusioned with Pétain. She had overheard someone say these young people had attached themselves to de Gaulle who was in London with the Free French. They were waiting for instructions from London. Until then, there was little going on other than subversive newspapers. She wished she could tell people in the south, most of them *attentistes* with their heads in the sand, just what it was like to live under the heel of the occupier. It would shock them and maybe galvanize them into some sort of action.

She had to wait for the young man to return, the old ladies said. When he finally arrived a few days later, she felt strong enough to leave. He drove her to a nearby village, where a tall church spire overhung a group of stone cottages, their shutters closed against the winter chill.

"Go to the *boulangerie* and speak to Simone," he said before driving off. "She's a friend of mine. She'll have a present for you."

In the bakery Alice and Evelyne were enveloped in the warm aroma of baked bread. She bought a small baguette and together she and Evelyne devoured, it standing in the lee of the building out of the clutches of the wind. In San Francisco, there would be crusty rolls or fresh bagels filled with cream cheese that squished as you bit into them. Did she remember that or was it a false memory, something she had dreamed of for so long that it had become real?

Simone led them down a winding street, pushed open a solid front door and led Alice and Evelyne inside. This time the home had better facilities; a proper toilet instead of some trees. Then there was a hot meal amongst a silent family who glanced at her and smiled shyly. She realized this meal had been for the family and they had shared it with her and

Evelyne, taking food off their own plates for a stranger. Heroism on a small scale, but heroism nevertheless. She felt overwhelmed with gratitude.

Once night had set in Simone took them to the railway station, Evelyne drooping with fatigue. The young woman pressed some documents into Alice's hand before walking away. Alice bought her ticket at the *guichet*, the ticket office, and sat in the waiting room to avoid the drafty platform. The hard benches, the sweet perfume of the wood fire and tobacco were better than the outside temperature. Someone opened a window, but that only made things worse as it picked up the acrid smoke from the trains. The window was sharply closed and the waiting passengers sat quietly, wrapped in their own thoughts. Alice felt that she was finally on her way to Nice.

Eventually, the train arrived. Late, always late, somebody mumbled. Never mind, everyone knew there was a shortage of coal and the rails somewhere along the line might have been damaged by bombs. A general rush, pushing and shoving and they were in, bundles distributed, food unwrapped and shared, a piece of hard-earned nougat for Evelyne, 'she is so good, Madame'. A railway restaurant car offered only day-old sandwiches and the usual ersatz coffee. Alice bought a cup and drank it standing in the aisle. Guards checked papers, looked askance at some of them but Alice's documentation seemed in order. The seats were hard and unforgiving but Alice and Evelyne slept as the train rattled on through the night. Finally, as morning broke into a glory of red banded cloud, they arrived in Nice.

Alice was disappointed with her first glimpse of the Mediterranean. She had expected it to be a forgiving blue and mild as milk-water, but instead it was grey and raged like a wounded fox. White foam slapped the foreshore and wind lifted grey froth and blew it across the streets and into the faces of people hurrying by.

Alice turned away from the sullen sea and sought out the American Consulate in avenue Gustav V. No, sorry, the young lady at the counter said. No one named Pothron had left a message.

"No message? Nothing? Are you sure?"

The woman shrugged. "No message, Madame."

So, there it was.

Emile had promised. If he was not here in Nice then he was dead and she had been fooling herself all along. She moved blindly away from the counter, brushing past shoulders and handbags until she and Evelyne were out in the chill air. Outside the Consulate she sat on a bench, too numb to care. It was only then that she allowed her tears to fall. A man stopped in front of her with a look of concern.

"... *êtes vous en difficulté*, Madame?"

For a moment she sat and watched his mouth. He was saying something to her but she could not work out what it was. Trouble? No trouble, she thought shaking her head, none that you could fix anyway. He walked away.

It was hard to concentrate, to decide what to do. They'd come so far on the vague hope that Emile was alive and had somehow got to the south of France. It had been the engine that had kept her walking through knee-deep snow drifts, pounding on strange doors hoping for a dry place to sleep and a crust of bread for Evelyne, trusting in strangers.

Now hope was gone. Alice did not know what to do – except to keep moving.

239

Another train journey, she decided, this time to Marseille. She was getting the hang of train stations and crowded railway carriages. She had quickly noticed that a tired wan-faced young woman with a fractious toddler was enough to allow her through with comparative ease. Inspectors checking papers on the train left her alone – women generally had a better time of it and one with a child even more so. Passengers gave her the best seats or left her alone. She realized with a start that Christmas had come and gone. Somewhere along her journey she had lost the New Year as well. She was on her way to another strange city, to Marseille, to another consulate with the mad hope that she might find Emile there, waiting for her.

At *Gare St Charles*, the main Marseille railway station, she handed her papers to the inspector at the barricade and they were handed back without comment. From the top of the station's majestic staircase she could see across to Vieux Port, the old harbor area and the two guardians of the harbor, Fort St Nicolas and Fort St Jean and out to the Mediterranean. The monumental stairway, flanked by stone columns, led down to la Canebière, the main street. She walked down and stood for a moment next to the bronze lion crouching over its prey. This was Marseille, February 1942, noisy, dirty and filled with shabby refugees just like her.

It had been a nautical city since the seventh century BC, when Phoenicians sailed the Mediterranean. Because of its position and the barrier of mountains close by, from which a fierce mistral wind blew, the summers were short. Marseille was therefore not a tourist town.

Instead it was a tough city of skullduggery and mischief; filled with refugees, transients, rough sailors and criminals of all stripes. Vieux Port, in particular, was a warren of winding alleyways and dark buildings housing prostitutes, smugglers, stranded Allied servicemen, resistance workers, Jews and others who wished to avoid the authorities. At every street corner frightened refugees stood, looking aimless and hungry. Alice recognized their haunted expressions and suspected her own face was equally ravaged.

She matched her pace to Evelyne's as they slowly made their way to the Consulate offices in Place Félix Baret, just off the Place de la Préfecture. The offices were in a handsome old building in a shady street where a long line of shabbily dressed people stood patiently. By questioning some of the more friendly-looking ones, she realized they were hoping for American visas or, more hopefully, an American passport. Alice secretly thanked her lucky stars that she had insisted on keeping her passport. All she needed now was official documentation for Evelyne and some sort of exit permit that would take her to Spain and, finally, back to America.

Pushing past the security guards, she walked into the hallway. The crowded waiting room was filled with stoic people and she realized, with a drop of her shoulders, that she would have to wait her turn.

The conversation in the line, once she joined its tail end, was about the idiocy of it all. To journey through France you needed a travel permit which she had, thanks to the man with the *gazogène.* Then you needed an exit visa to get out of France. But it was almost impossible to get one of those, someone warned.

If you wanted an exit visa you had to apply to Vichy and then your name went before the Kundt Commission, a branch of the Gestapo. Being on a list, any list, was dangerous. It could mean arrest and worse. Anyway, someone said, if you wanted to plead your cause you needed a pass to get into the town of Vichy where the provisional government was situated.

Then the Spanish would not let you in without documentation. It was all too hard.

Alice sorted through the information she heard. You had to get a visa to exit from France and then an entry visa for Spain. Then you had to have a Spanish transit visa because they did not want refugees milling about in Spain. You could not get a transit visa until you had a Portuguese entry visa and that was not obtainable unless you had a booked and paid-for transatlantic passenger ticket. By the time Alice had worked all this out her head was spinning.

It became obvious from the advice she heard in that line outside the American Consulate, that a French exit visa was not going to be available. But, if she could just get the entry visa into Spain, she would find a way to get out of France before the Nazis occupied the whole country, as was inevitable.

CHAPTER 27

For the sake of the thirty-six concealed saints,
God preserves the world, even if the rest of
humanity has degenerated to
the level of barbarism.

- The Kabbalah

Alice and Evelyne spent their first day in Marseille in front of the American Embassy. The line snaked down the street and round the corner, a long row of the tired and helpless. Although they were given numbered place cards, which meant they could go and get a meal or a quick sleep, few fell out of the line.

Evelyne had been remarkably docile, leaning against her mother's knee – the picture of exhaustion. She never complained, even when she must have been almost as hungry and as tired as her mother. There were other children. Most were older than Evelyne and Alice wondered at their fate.

Night drew in and the Embassy doors closed. Still the people waited, but Alice could take no more. She stumbled to a bench nearby. To sit in comfort, to take the weight off her aching feet, seemed like heaven. A man stopped in front of her as she brushed the snow off the bench and prepared to settle for the night.

"This is no place for a child, Madame. You two will freeze to death out here."

"I have nowhere to go, Monsieur."

"Go to Vieux Port. There are a number of hotels where you can stay." When he saw her hesitate he continued. "Madame, it is better than freezing on the street." From his pocket he took out a small pad and wrote something on it. He handed the note to Alice together with a few coins. "Go to this address in Vieux Port. It's not a very grand place but at least you'll be warm."

"If I go I may lose my place in the line tomorrow morning."

"If you stay you will die."

Alice found the place easily enough. As the stranger suggested, the place was not very grand. The *concierge* did not ask Alice to register on the card index nor did she ask for documents. She pointed to the stairs and a basic room on the second floor where Alice and Evelyne could sleep.

Best described as a *maisons de passé* or *maisons de rendez-vous,* Alice discovered next morning the rooms were let by the hour to men who brought with them their own female companion. It was noisy, but it was warm and the bed was clean. They ate breakfast at a small café nearby and rejoined the line outside the American Embassy.

By the second day, people's faces started to look familiar. The thin woman with an old astrakhan coat so worn in places the bare leather poked through. A couple, elderly, the woman sniffling her tears into a small lace handkerchief. A tall grey-haired man anxiously clutched a leather brief-case. Two young women, sisters perhaps, were holding hands. Conversation gathered momentum as the sun rose and a warm day stretched out before them.

It was three days later, with nights spent at the *maisons de rendez-vous,* that Alice was finally ushered into an office.

"I want to go home," was all Alice could think of saying. Standing in the line she had tried out different scenarios, different words but in the end it came down to a five-word sentence filled with longing and hope – I want to go home.

"Are you alone?" The official asked.

She pointed to Evelyne, nodded and told him a little of her story, holding out her American passport. He listened sympathetically.

"The only way out is through Lisbon in Portugal. Now, this is how you do it." He began writing a list. "When you get home where will you go?" he asked. "What will you do? I can loan you some money but we need a guarantee that you won't be a burden on the state. You must have a sponsor."

She had a sudden thought. "Jacques," she said. "Jacques Laffont in Beverley Hills. He'll vouch for me."

She had not thought of Jacques for a long time. She remembered his cheery good nature and his love for Emile, whom he called 'his little brother'. Jacques was probably a success now, his dream of being a hairdresser to the stars quite possible, given his charm and expertise. She wondered how different her life would have been had Emile decided to go with Jacques to Hollywood, instead of taking her on a vacation to France. She felt sick with the realization that, had they gone to Hollywood, Emile would still be alive.

It was a long and frustrating process. First, her passport was updated and Evelyne included, then a wait for the Spanish entry visa. She had been advised by a woman standing behind her in one of the lines that Cooks travel agency was issuing false passenger tickets for non-existent ships, supposedly leaving from Lisbon. At two hundred francs it was a bargain.

Another day and a night standing in a line but, with the passenger ticket in her handbag, Alice felt reasonably sure she would be granted a Portuguese visa. By the time the Portuguese visa came through the Spanish one had lapsed. So the merry-go-round started again.

In the line, she had heard a few stories of the difficulties of getting a valid passport. Some of the embassies were issuing false passports to help people get out of France. For example, if you were stateless, as the Jews were, then you could get a pink Czech 'interim' passport. The Chinese embassy staff was also issuing passports. Someone roguishly suggested that the Chinese writing said; 'This person is under no circumstances to be allowed into China'. Never mind, the Portuguese authorities probably could not read Chinese anyway. She felt blessed she had the genuine thing in her handbag.

She heard whispers about an American called Varian Fry, who was helping stranded intellectuals and artists to leave France. Many being helped were stateless, after having had their citizenship revoked on the order of the Germans, and were at great risk of being deported to the camps.

Never had she felt more thankful for her naturalization than standing in that line in Marseille and hearing the terrible stories floating around her.

The last document she needed was the French exit visa and, she had been warned, it was not advisable to apply for one. But someone had hinted at another way to get out of France, over the mountains.

A lifetime later, or so it felt, Alice was on the Marseille railway station waiting for a train to take her and Evelyne to Perpignan, a town close to the border.

She felt loaded with documents, except for the all-important exit visa. She mentally ticked off the list. She had some French francs given to her by the Embassy. She was warned it was illegal to take money out of France so she unpicked the seam inside her valise, stuffed the franc notes in and sewed it up again. Emile's passport was also in her valise, but that was only for memory's sake.

"When you get to Spain you must get the visa stamped," the official explained. "Without that *entrada* stamp you will be arrested as an illegal and sent back."

The train was late and she went into the *Buffet de la Gare* where she and Evelyne shared a cup of hot *café national* and a sandwich. When the train finally arrived there was the usual scramble by frustrated passengers, pushing and tumbling and finally settling with much wriggling and elbow gouging. Alice found a seat next to a peasant woman who carried a large bag of vegetables and a live chicken by its legs. Evelyne sat quietly on her mother's lap, intrigued by the upside-down chicken that gave an occasional futile squawk. Alice fell into an uncomfortable sleep, her head throbbing with pain.

As the train pulled out of *Gare St Charles,* Alice looked back at the great grey docks stretching from Bassin de la Joliette to Bassin du Président Wilson. She caught a glimpse of Vieux Port where they had slept and then Marseille was gone. They left behind the limestone hills and traveled through the low lands of the Languedoc with its pattern of squat sandbars and swamps and its stampeding wild ponies; along the coastline, the Mediterranean fierce and white-capped on her left. At Sete, a port town with fishing boats jostling for space in the canals, the peasant woman, puffing and red-cheeked, lifted her black-clad bulk and wheezed out of the carriage and on to the platform where the chicken gave a resigned and final cluck.

At last Alice was able to get to the window where the air seemed a little cooler. Was it hot in here, she wondered, or is it just me? And yet she was shivering. The five-hour trip passed slowly, like a long drawn-out nightmare, all elongated shapes with faces coming towards her and then receding. Later, she remembered getting off at Narbonne, the echoing station, dank and dirty, and changing trains for Perpignan. At Perpignan she was directed to the tram station for Canet Plage where the American official had advised her to stay. The official at the Embassy had suggested that Madame LeBreton, the owner of the *Hotel du Tennis,* was someone who could help her, who would know how to get into Spain without an exit visa.

At Canet Plage, she walked through the wide streets bordered by houses with red Spanish tiles, vaguely reminding her of California. At the *Hotel du Tennis* she would rest for a few days, gathering her strength for the final part of the journey.

Was Evelyne getting heavier? It felt like she was carrying a log of wood. Alice's muscles stung, her head ached and her vision began to blur. Evelyne's childish prattle was a solid whine that drilled through her foggy brain. She staggered and someone took her arm and helped her along the wide street to the hotel. Her breath was a fireball in her chest.

Finally, she entered the hotel foyer. A kindly-looking *concierge* looked up and smiled. She just had time to put Evelyne down when the air became fuzzy.

She had reached the limit of her strength and was in no fit state to take the final steps to freedom. It looked like the end of the road.

*In the background the
Hotel du Tennis, Canet Plage, 1940*

CHAPTER 28

We never know how high we are
'til we are asked to rise
and then if we are true to plan
our statures touch the skies
- Emily Dickinson

The winter gave its last few grumpy puffs and spring elbowed the cold aside. Mimosa yellowed the hillsides and the warm air helped to renew Alice's energy. After a week, she was finally ready to tackle the last obstacle to freedom.

But the obstacle was the Pyrenees Mountains, a truly formidable barrier.

She had to hurry now. Her documents would shortly expire. There was no more time to hang around the *Hotel du Tennis* in Canet Plage, however comfortable Mme LeBreton had made her stay. Alice packed her valise, accepted a small food package from the *concierge* and took the tram back to Perpignan. From there they would take the train to Banyuls-sur-Mer, the closest town to the Pyrenees.

Perpignan was a charming town. Wide boulevards were lined with palm trees. It bustled with people drinking wine at sidewalk cafes or hurrying along the streets; patched clothes and hats firmly stuck on heads. As in the north, shoes were always the worse for wear. Once again, Alice saw there was adversity even in the 'unoccupied' south.

Had Alice known, Perpignan was also filled with *résistants* proud of their Catalan heritage of never bowing to invaders. Intrigue and secrets oozed out of every hotel and bistro, snaked around corners and settled in many hearts. For this reason, the crowds were closely watched by *gendarmes* and plainclothes men with intense eyes. The Gestapo knew that Perpignan was also the springboard for escape to Spain, and they watched carefully.

The railway line ran south from Perpignan through a number of tunnels before the border. Alice had originally planned to take the simplest route, by train to Port-Vendres and on to Cerbère. From there she would walk past the old cemetery, up the hill and over into Spain. Mme LeBreton explained to her that route was the easier one, but lately the authorities had begun to watch it very closely. Now it was being guarded by diligent French *gardes mobiles* and escapees had to take a more circuitous route. They were now crossing on what was an old smugglers route further to the west where, unfortunately, the mountains were higher, the snow deeper and the climb more treacherous. It meant that, instead of leaving from Cerbère, the refugees had to leave from Banyuls-sur-Mer.

Alice and Evelyne had been at the Perpignan railway station since before dawn. Passengers were beginning to get restless; cursing the war, muttering under their breath at the disruption of their lives, of the lateness of trains in general and this one, in particular.

At last, the train smoked into the station and passengers pushed and jockeyed for a place. Once on board, Evelyne was alive with curiosity. So much to see and to remark on that Alice soon found her mind awash with childish questions without the strength

251

or the knowledge to answer. As the train moved through a little canyon and on to high ground she glimpsed the Mediterranean, which today was blue and calm. They raced through a tunnel where the train roared and spat cinders then stopped at Colliourre. Vendors strode the platform and passengers alighted, stretching their legs until the inspector's whistle blew its shrill demand and they were on their way again. Another short dark sulphurous tunnel and, as they exited the darkness, she saw a small turquoise lake, a tranquil bowl of glacial water filled from the icy upper reaches of the Pyrenees.

In the afternoon they arrived at Banyuls-sur-Mer, so close to the mountains she could almost touch them. Alice's heart dropped. They looked cold and sullen. Unwelcome. Could she actually walk over those threatening crags to Spain, and with a small child? Alice began to have grave doubts.

She found a small bistro where they were served a nourishing meal. As Alice used the bread she'd been given to wipe the edges of the plate the proprietor sat down opposite her. His questioning eyes scanned her face.

"A refugee? You want to get over?" he asked quietly, jerking his thumb at the mountains.

She nodded.

He pulled out a cigarette, lit it and took a long draw, surveying Evelyne who sat next to Alice, her eyes wide with interest.

"With the child? Alone?"

Again she nodded.

He gave a short bark of laughter. "Either you are mad-crazy or desperate."

"Probably both," she grinned.

He called to a waiter and soon two cups of coffee, two glasses of cognac and a glass of milk for Evelyne were set down on the table. He told her of the old smugglers' route, *le route Lister,* named after Enrique Lister, he explained, a Spanish military man who fled up this defile in 1939. Not easy, he said, you can walk it but, with a child, he looked dubious.

He spoke of the workers from a vineyard on the outskirts of town, and of a small hut on the upper slope where she could rest. On a high plateau there were seven pine trees, head for them, he said, and keep them on your right. High up there was another vineyard. Once you pass that you are nearly there, nearly at the peak. He spoke of the advantages of the route, that large parts were sheltered by overhanging rock. What he did not say, and what Alice found out the hard way, was that, over eons, the pathway had been scoured out of the side of the mountain and fell, almost vertically, to the valleys below.

Alice found a room at a small inn that overlooked the lower slopes of the vineyards. From the window she would see the lines of grapes, their rows straight as arrows, pointing towards the upper hills where soon she would be walking. The man at the bistro had said she should join the vineyard workers before dawn, mingle with them until she got to the upper edges. The border guards watch the workers, he warned, so blend in and take as little luggage as possible. Someone walking with a suitcase and a fur coat was sure to attract the wrong kind of attention. Alice assured him she had neither.

It was before dawn the next morning when Alice and Evelyne left the comfort of the inn and joined the group of workers steadily making its way to the vineyard. Each man carried a *musette* or haversack over a hunched shoulder. Her battered valise was inconspicuous. As they slipped in with the workers there were a few whispered, *"bonjour"* and *"bonne chance"* but most of the workers just made room for her as they walked along the dew-wet cobbled street.

As she and Evelyne tried to blend in with the workers, Alice wondered what Emile would have thought of his quiet little wife who never questioned or criticized and who never made any of the big decisions. His had been a restless spirit, never settling, never quite knowing where he belonged. Before they had married, he and Jacques Laffont had moved apartments nine times in two years. In the ten years of their marriage, they had lived in New York, Boston and San Francisco. Emile always had plans and those plans involved a lot of moving around. Had they got back to America this time, he would no doubt have changed their lives yet again. She had always kept quiet and gone along with what he wanted. But now it was different. Now she was on her own, and she had better come up to scratch or they would die. It was a fearful responsibility.

At the edge of the vineyard, a worker pointed wordlessly to a narrow path. He gave her a big grin and a thumbs-up as she walked on, through the thin beech trees with their white trunks like mottled fingers pointing at the sky. Beyond them a few small pines looked like forgotten Christmas trees, their branches rimed with frost. The granite boulders were the size of San Francisco trams, mossy and glistening in the last weak rays of a sickle moon.

Soon the path became tortuous. Her thin-soled shoes slipped on the rocks and once her ankle twisted. Evelyne gave a soft whine and Alice picked her up, this time finding her footing with more care. She started to count the steps, promising herself that when she got to one hundred she would put Evelyne down and the child would have to walk. It was almost as if she was back in Paron at the water pump. *Un, deux, trois …*

Sunrise slipped over the horizon like silk soaked in blood. It burst across the Mediterranean on her left, the light lying flat along the sea. As daylight flooded the path she got into a rhythm; one hundred paces – slip – slide, pick Evelyne up and carry her, another hundred paces, sit down, rest.

Three hours after starting out they came to a large grey boulder, exactly as the bistro owner had described. She sat down, her back to its mossy façade, thankful for the respite. Together, mother and child shared a little of the water, bread and cheese. They lay back and Alice wondered if the sky had ever been quite so blue, the clouds so glitteringly white. She was fortunate, for once the weather held and the mountain was bathed in sharp sunlight, although above her on the slopes of the mountain the snow lay thick.

After the boulder, the way got steeper, along slopes of rocky scree gouged by ancient glaciers, then onto a series of long hairpin bends where she could see only that part of the path directly above her. She plodded on, under overhanging cliffs with needle-fine waterfalls making the path muddy and treacherous.

Although the sun still shone it was colder now, the air thin and sharp. Blisters began to form on her feet and her ankles ached. She needed to rest, to ease the muscles in her legs and the trembling in her arms from carrying Evelyne.

When they came upon it, the deserted hut was exactly where the bistro owner had said. They could keep walking but Alice felt her strength ebbing, her breath coming in hot gasps and her arms numb from the burden of the child. Soon it would be night and this was as good a place to sleep as any. The straw on the floor smelt rancid but Alice raked the top layer aside and they lay down and soon fell asleep.

Welcomed by a bright morning, they tumbled out of the hut into the icy air that cleansed the mountains like an airbrush. The last of the early mist gathered in valleys below and above them the peaks stood out clear and sharp. Invigorated by a night's sleep and a few bites of bread for breakfast, Alice began to walk again but, when they came to a fork in the path, she faltered. She was sure the bistro owner had not mentioned this. Which path should she take? She did not know.

In a sweep of fear, Alice realized how easily they could get lost in the mountains. She had deliberately avoided thinking about the dangers and pitfalls of going it alone. Stupid, stupid! Just how arrogant can you be? She did not know which path to follow, could not tell which one would lead to safety and which back into France and possibly into the hands of the *gardes mobiles*. Never had she felt so alone.

She sat down under a scrubby tree with Evelyne next to her. Below them the Mediterranean shone; above her the mountain pierced the morning sky. The peaks looked menacing and Alice shuddered at the thought of their bodies lying there until someone stumbled over them in the summer.

She looked up at the towering cliffs ahead of her. It was no good. They were not going to make it. In despair, Alice began to weep.

It was then that she heard them, walking up the path towards her. Too tired to move, she waited to be discovered. She heard soft voices and, peering round the tree, saw they were not men from the border patrol but people dressed much like herself, ragged, hunched and probably just as cold and as hungry as she was. She stood up. There was no need to say anything.

The guide looked her over, looked up at the mountain crest and shook his head. He was obviously of the opinion that here was a very crazy woman, walking alone with a child in this hostile place. He gestured to her to sit down. Wordlessly, he handed her a pair of espadrilles from the number he had hanging round his neck. As Alice exchanged her sandals for the rope-soled canvas shoes, she noticed that every person in the group was similarly shod. The *alpargatas* would make it easier to walk up the narrow rock-strewn path, the guide said.

When she stood up, the guide took Evelyne from her and beckoned Alice to follow. They began to walk in single-file with the soft fall of their footsteps, the occasional rattle of a stone, a muffled curse the only sound. The guide sensibly refused to allow Evelyne to walk. She would slow them down, he said, with some justification. So, between them; Alice, the guide and the fitter of the young people in the party, Evelyne was carried up the mountain.

As they walked the air grew thinner, harder to breathe. They emerged from the tree line and the snow piled up around them in brilliant heaps, almost waist-high. Soon their espadrilles were wet through and still they trudged on.

The smuggler's path ran parallel to the main road but was concealed by an overhang. Once they heard the approach of the *gardes mobiles,* the motorized border guards, just above them. Alice placed her hand gently over Evelyne's mouth. A word, a whimper from her, would have meant discovery. They heard voices, some laughter, a steady stream of urine hitting stones and then they were gone.

The group of refugees padded along as silently as they could. Hearing the *gardes mobiles* just above them had been a shock. The whines and grumbles of the escapees, the impatient admonitions from the guide that 'if a woman and a small child can do it, then you can as well', had been silenced and they walked on, keeping their own pain and exhaustion to themselves.

The path became slippery and narrow, a precipitous fall of several hundred feet to a small lake below. They continued walking slowly, this time taking greater care to ensure that no stones rolled underfoot and sent them plunging down. This time it was the guide who carried Evelyne, instructing the child to hold onto his hair from her royal seat on his shoulders. Alice edged along, her back pressed to the cliff as if bolted with chains. She dared not look down lest she lose her equilibrium and fall.

The cold wind howled and blustered as if trying to pluck them from the narrow pathway and hurl them into the valley below. And finally, just as she felt she was getting to the end of her strength, they reached the summit and stood for a moment in the crystalline splendor. Below them was the radiant blue of the Mediterranean and on the other side steep cliffs fell into a valley carpeted with wild flowers. Even in her state of near-total exhaustion Alice could appreciate the beauty.

But there was still a long way to go. From now on they would be on the warm side of the Pyrenees and the difference in temperature was magical and provided new hope. There was a sense of the journey almost completed. The path led downwards, winding through scrub and spring flowers. Alice's feet, bruised and blistered, were automatically finding their way through the scree that slid and shifted and slithered underfoot.

And there it was; a small town resting on the edge of the Mediterranean. Port-Bou. It had to be Port-Bou in Spain. It radiated safety and somehow she had to find the strength to walk those last few miles.

"Border control. Border control."

It became her mantra. Get the *entrada* stamp at the border control or you will be arrested and sent back.

The end was so close and yet her feet could hardly obey her brain. They slapped down sending tendrils of dust into the air. A few more steps. That is all it would take. Just a few. Step. Step. See that tree there? Make it to that tree then find something else to aim for. Now that rock? See that rock?

And then she was there. It had been nearly thirty-six hours since she had left Banyuls-sur-Mer, most of it spent climbing the mountain.

Just above the town the guide called a halt. This was where he would leave the group, he said. He could go no further without risking arrest. Alice took Evelyne from his arms, uncertain how to thank this *passeur* who had rescued them from the mountains. He did not seem to want thanks, just a handshake from the exhausted group and then he began his return through the Pyrenees to guide another group of refugees to safety.

At the border control, a bored man in a green uniform bent his cockaded hat over her American passport and other papers. Stamp. Stamp. He shoved them back at her and pointed out the railway station where she could get a train to Lisbon. The main group was taking the train to Barcelona and thence to Madrid. They would end up in Gibraltar to be repatriated. It was time to say goodbye. She gave each a heartfelt hug.

"*Merci, merci beaucoup.*"

Those words had fallen from her lips many, many times since leaving Paron, but never with such fervor. She would never see them again but they would be in her prayers for the rest of her life.

They received her gratitude with shy grins and left her at the station.

CHAPTER 29

It is not the mountain we conquer,
but ourselves.

- Sir Edmund Hillary

Alice was clearly in no fit state to take the train.
Even the man at the ticket office could see that.
Instead, he sent her to the local hotel, the Fonda de
Francia, where she booked a room for the night. After
a meal of orange slices, a few figs, goat's cheese and
the ubiquitous bread she and Evelyne fell into the
comfort of the hard bed and slept for almost twelve
hours.

Port-Bou still showed signs of the Civil War
which had ended in 1939. It had suffered bombing by
Italian aircraft and bomb sites, especially in the area
of the docks, were still like open sores. Alice had not
seen such damage, even in France, and the desolation
shocked her.

In this shell-shocked little fishing town, Alice
thought she was safe from the Germans without
realizing that the hotel Fonda de Francia was the
favored watering hole for special services. This
included the Gestapo posing as shipping agents.
Nevertheless they did not seem particularly
interested in one small woman and her peevish
toddler.

It was only now, as she sat on the veranda
looking out towards the flattened docks, that Alice
tried to grasp what she had undertaken. It had been
foolish to try it alone, she now recognized that. She

had been totally ignorant of the immensity of the mountains, their bleak wildness, sharp cliffs and precipitous falls. How easy it would have been for her and Evelyne to have become lost, to have fallen or to have disappeared into a snow-filled crevasse. She shuddered at the mere thought of it.

But they had made it. In Paron, she and Evelyne had lived through harsh times. They had made an almost miraculous escape with the help of Lulu and Edward. Together she and her little girl had journeyed, mostly on foot, through a winter-riven France. They had got to Marseille, where she succeeded in obtaining all the right documents even though it had meant standing in the cold street day after day. Then together they had climbed a mountain. It had taken them almost two days but here they were, in Spain, with a fighting chance of finally making it to Lisbon and then back to America.

It would be Evelyne's third birthday in just a few months and it looked as if they would celebrate it in freedom. The idea buoyed Alice up and gave her the strength to ask for a train timetable.

"No timetable," is what she thought the receptionist said. He laughed and she wondered if a timetable was something out of the ordinary, like asking for a zebra. Perhaps it was.

She went to the train station and caught a westbound train to San Sebastian. From there another train would take her along the vastness of northern Spain and to Portugal. They were finally on the last leg of the journey, just one more border crossing and she would be safe.

The train crabbed along the lower reaches of the Pyrenees and through what was essentially a broken country. Everywhere she looked there were the tailings of civil war; burned-out villages, empty fields, broken trees and broken people. On the train were travelers whose scoured faces held the memory of what civil war had done to their country. At each station small vagabonds ran alongside the train begging for food and she was heart-piercingly reminded of Emile and his beggar days in Paris. The women walking alongside the children were like twisted crows, their broken shoes shuffling along the platform, burdened by a new-laid poverty, suffering etched on each face, on each bent body.

At San Sebastian she caught another train, the carriage reeking of garlic and rancid oil, that sped through a hot dry region west towards the Portuguese border. Orange orchards gave way to olive trees and red roofs. She no longer paid much attention. Her mind was focused on Lisbon, on the American Legation and on final sanctuary.

As the train drew closer to Portugal, Alice no longer noticed the cork plantations, the cacti that lined the rail track, the pale houses and the dark people. Her mind was so intent on Lisbon that, when the train finally came to a standstill at the Oriente Station in the heart of *Parque das Nações*, she sat hardly able to move for fear the dream would end and she would wake up and find herself still in France.

It was all so different; a cacophony of traffic after the silent streets of France, the shops filled with luxuries she barely remembered, like soap and food and books. The people who hurried past her did not have the same strained look as those in France. There were no *gendarmes* or German soldiers on every street corner demanding papers. No hateful red and black posters on the walls announcing new restrictions, new reprisals. Above all, there were no swastikas hanging from flagpoles. In those first hours in Lisbon, she began the long slow task of letting go and allowing freedom to soak into her.

It was too late for the Legation so Alice looked for a room at a hotel near the station. The concierge shook her head. So many foreigners, she indicated. No rooms anywhere. The second hotel had the same message. Lisbon was awash with refugees and there were no rooms available. Finally, after the fifth or was it the sixth hotel, the manager took pity on Alice and a drooping Evelyne and showed them to a small room, hardly bigger than a broom cupboard.

Alice put Evelyne down on the bed and fell next to her. They slept for an hour and woke up hungry. Alice poured some water from a large jug into the porcelain basin and began to wash, first Evelyne's face and then her own. The soap was so smooth, like silk, not the coarse grey stuff she had used in Paron. Her first taste of luxury was a piece of soap that foamed when she used it.

They walked out into the busy street to buy food. She could not believe the people were walking with such confidence. Even the air about her seemed affable. It was late into the evening; past curfew time. Were they not afraid? Of course, she was in Portugal, not France.

Alice was entranced by the quantity and variety of food in the stores. She bought some bread, real bread, soft and white like candy-floss. With a few of her remaining American dollars, she bought butter and a small pot of real jam. At a candy store, she gave in to temptation and bought a little slab of chocolate.

One night, she thought, one night in the hotel and then in the morning to the American Legation. She had her passport and a fake ticket for a fake ship. She would present these to the officials at the Legation and hope for the best. With any luck she would soon be on board a ship, a real one, or a plane bound for New York. Once there, she would make her way to Los Angeles and find Jacques Laffont. He would know what to do.

As she lay on the bed in the small hotel on a busy Lisbon street with Evelyne nestled in beside her, Alice could see that her life had fallen into several clearly defined episodes, like separate chapters in a book. The first chapter was her childhood in the orphanage, where she had experienced a slavery of sorts and where she had stayed until her twentieth year. Then there were the years in New York, as *tante* Louise's maid – another sort of servitude. When she met Emile she experienced an entirely different chapter, one filled with love and happiness. The events in Paron were ones she did not want to think about but also made up a chapter of slavery in the story of her life. Now, she faced the last chapter of her story, returning to America without Emile and a life of loss and sadness.

All these different lives crammed into one lifetime, she thought, as she fell asleep. How strange.

In the early morning, an orange streetcar bore Alice and Evelyne through the traffic jams and along the streets of Lisbon. The morning air was filled with the scent of flowers and wood smoke. The streetcar clattered down steep hills that reminded Alice of San Francisco and to the front door of the American Legation, a large white building in Avenue Duque de Loulé. Across the road there were palm trees, rotund with crowns of blazing green, the sort Alice had last seen in California. It brought the ache of home so much closer.

They alighted from the tram, Alice still shaky and still bone-weary, and made their way to the imposing front door where a young black soldier stood guard. Everything about him shone; his boots and belt, his brass buttons and his large smiling face.

"Good morning, Ma'am. I'm Jerome. How can I help you?"

Her legs felt weak, her heart pounded with an irregular beat. "I've come from France and I want to go home," she said, her lips beginning to tremble.

"I'm sure you do, Ma'am," he said. "Now, don't you worry one little bit. We'll see that you get back to good ole US of A. You have an American passport?"

"Yes," she said.

She handed the passport to him. He opened it, scrutinized it, looked at her and then looked at the passport again.

"Mrs. Pothron? Mrs. Alice Pothron?" He pronounced it as the Americans did. "That's not a usual Yankee kind of name," he said.

Alice was in the entrance foyer of what had to be the most beautiful building in the world. She hung onto the door jamb afraid her legs would give way before she had finally crossed the threshold.

"My, my, you look all in, Mrs. Pothron. I think you better come inside while I go find somebody for you."

He gently took Evelyne's hand and led them to a row of wooden chairs.

"Now ya'll wait here and I'll be back in a shake," he said.

"My passport?" she called.

"Don't you worry your pretty little head, Mrs. Pothron. It'll be safe with me."

"But where are you going?"

"To find someone you need to see."

She slumped down, rested her head on the back of the chair. Around her she heard the bustle of people coming and going, hushed whispers, the scrape of chairs as one couple left from in front of a desk and another took their place. There were so many, like herself, who had escaped from France and were now trying to get to America, each pleading their cause to the officials. At each desk a brass lamp shone on inadequate papers presented by anxious fingers. She closed her eyes. God, she was worn out. She felt as old as Methuselah's wife. Her heart was beating so fast, so erratically it felt like it was about to jump out of her blouse.

This Jerome fellow must be going to fetch an official who would have to be told the whole sorry story. She would begin by telling him how she and Emile had gone to France for a vacation and had gotten caught up in the dreadful happenings. She would have to explain that Emile had been captured and sent to Germany and that he was dead. They would hear how she had escaped over the Pyrenees with their child. In her tired brain, she began to form the words into sentences and then into paragraphs that made some sort of sense.

The man, Jerome, was taking so long. What was the problem?

Then a shadow fell between her and the light. It was Jerome, his black face split by a smile.

"Here you are, Mrs. Pothron, a late Christmas present."

She looked up. The sun was in her eyes. It must be the sun for suddenly her vision blurred. She screamed and reached out her hands to the small grey-haired man standing smiling before her.

It was Emile.

EPILOGUE

> I think the only appropriate attitude to such
> coincidences is to not even try to explain them.
> Anyway, I am too ignorant to explain them,
> and too smart to deny them.
>
> — Viktor Frankl

Alice and Emile Pothron were finally reunited after their separate and harrowing ordeals. Staff took a special interest in them and the amazing coincidence that led them to be in the offices of the American Legation in Lisbon on the same day. They arranged for the Pothron family to stay in a hotel and for a doctor to attend to Alice.

The news was not good.

She was diagnosed with a chronic heart condition and advised to take special care for the rest of her life. The diagnosis did not matter. She had accomplished what she had set out to do – ensure the survival of her beloved child. In the quiet moments, as she lay in bed recovering from her ordeal, Alice had time to look back on the past months. She realized that although Evelyne had relied totally on her mother for survival, so the ideal of her child's continued existence gave Alice the strength and courage to go on until they both reached safety. Without Evelyne she would probably still be in Paron, still a slave to the German forces in her house.

There would have been no reason to live and every reason to allow circumstances to overwhelm her.

While Alice recuperated and Emile got to know his little daughter, he told Alice about his escape from Val de Grace and wondered if Dr Delavierre had managed to get others out before the men were deported to Germany. He spoke of the year in the 'free' south when he had hidden from the Vichy authorities, of the kind people who had helped him and of the work he had finally found. She held him and they both wept as he spoke of his journey to Paron. He said he had seen the Germans in their house and had come to the erroneous conclusion that his family was dead.

If only she had known. If only she had looked out the window at that moment, everything would have been different.

Under the false name of Yves Dumont, he had travelled south through occupied France. At the demarcation line, he said, he had been assisted by seasoned *passeurs* and had finally landed up in Montluçon in what was called the free zone, although he had found it not free at all. He had spent a few days in Montluçon walking around, mapping in his mind the various engineering and chemical works that were obviously supplying the Germans. Then he had moved on.

He told Alice he took the train south until he reached Toulouse. It was there he remembered that the Hispano-Suiza automotive and engineering company had a factory in Tarbes, just south of Toulouse. As a young boy, Emile had served part of his apprenticeship at the Hispano-Suiza factory in Paris. He needed work and the Hispano-Suiza factory was only seventy miles away.

Extremely skilled at what he did and in dire need of a job, Emile visited M. Henri Garnier, deputy director of manufacturing, who was pleased to have such an able young man on his staff, even if his documents were a little suspect.

Garnier had vigorously opposed the Armistice and had tried, in vain, to go to North Africa from where he could get to London and join the Free French. When he was stopped, he reluctantly resumed his work at the Tarbes manufacturing plant.

In 1940 Vichy was encouraging aircraft companies to resume work after the defeat and, when collaboration became the norm, to build planes for the Luftwaffe. Hispano-Suiza was allowed to continue the manufacture of aircraft engines, in particular for the Dewoitine D.520 fighter aircraft, but on a one-to-one basis, one plane for the limited French Air Force and one for the Luftwaffe, until later when the ratio climbed to one-to-five.

At Tarbes, Henri Garnier headed a small team of employees who secretly sabotaged production at the plant, resulting in low productivity. As an engineer, he knew how to change plans very slightly so that the Dewoitines delivered to the Germans would fly for a limited number of hours before faults would permanently ground the airplanes. Manufacture was under German supervision, Emile told Alice, so resistance in the factory became a cat-and-mouse affair.

Towards the end of the year, Emile made his way to Spain, arriving in Lisbon in September 1941. In his head, he had a mass of information about German troop movements in the occupied zone, the location of gas supply depots as well as the strategic topography of France; the bridges, the railway lines and other vulnerable locations both in the occupied and the 'free' zones. He also had information about escape routes and the people who would help escapees in the future – none of which he could commit to paper. More importantly, he had accurate information about the Dunlop tire factory, as well as other strategic manufacturing plants in Montluçon. He had seen a fertilizer factory in Toulouse where explosives were being manufactured for the Germans. He also had detailed information on the Tarbes factory and its rather meager output.

In Lisbon, Emile had stayed at the Hotel Algarve and met a personable young Frenchman called Jean Moulin. Moulin guided Emile to Mr. L H Mortimore, a local British businessman who, he understood, had secret connections to Donald Darling and Jack Beevor of the British Embassy and, through them, to London. Mortimore interviewed Emile over several days, asking perceptive questions of the young man. He promised that the information would go to 'the right people'.

Between visiting Mr. Mortimore and the American Legation in Avenue Duque de Loulé, Emile spent some time with Jean Moulin. It was only much later Emile discovered that Moulin was an important figure in the French Resistance until his death by torture in July 1943. Emile would always remember the few days he spent talking to this charismatic young man before Moulin flew to London to meet Charles de Gaulle.

Alice was not as forthcoming about her experiences as Emile. He never knew of the gang-rape and the miscarriage that followed. There are some things wives do not reveal to their husbands. It was sufficient that they were now together again and would soon, with the help of the Legation, be on their way to New York.

The last act of generosity by the Legation staff was to help the family obtain berths on the *SS Drottningholm*, a Swedish charter ship used by the American, British, French and German governments for the exchange of diplomats, journalists, prisoners of war and others.

On 22 June 1942, two weeks after Evelyne's third birthday, the Pothron family finally departed from a still-seething Europe. They were bound for New York.

The Atlantic was the arena for fierce sea battles between German U-boats and Allied convoys taking much-needed supplies to Britain. The journey from Lisbon was tense as passengers could not be certain that a U-boat *Kapitäne* would honor their diplomatic status even though they steamed fully lighted and with the white sides of the ship painted with the words 'Diplomat – Sverige'.

They journeyed through bad weather and Evelyne was seasick for much of the time. Alice fed her thin slices of orange until the child was on her feet once again.

On the morning of 30 June 1942, passengers rushed up to the open deck cheering and waving. In the distance, they could see the Statue of Liberty proudly holding the flame of freedom that shone through the morning mist. They lay at anchor outside the harbor for most of the day while the American Coastguard boarded to inspect the ship and the passenger's documents. Then the ship's engines began to throb again and she moved slowly past the Statue of Liberty and towards the pier.

That was when Alice and Emile saw the SS *Normandie.*

She had been seized by the American government and designated a troop-carrying ship. On

9 February 1942 work had begun eviscerating her for the conversion. Now she lay on her side at Pier 88, a carcass ravished to death by flames when workers accidently (or intentionally) set her alight. Her gracious lines were still visible in spite of the flame damage.

"Oh, Emile," Alice said.

They held each other and cradled their three-year-old daughter between them. Their lives had come full circle, from the *Normandie* of their dreams to this awful dying hulk. It seemed like a metaphor; the luxury and ease with which they had left New York in June 1938 and the sad circumstances of their return, almost to the day, four momentous years later.

The *Drottningholm* slid gracefully to the pier. Messenger ropes were tossed to the stevedores and she was pulled alongside. Great hawsers held the white ship to the quay as the crew lowered a gangplank and passengers walked on to dry land.

Alice, Emile and Evelyne Pothron were finally home.

BIBLIOGRAPHY

Aubrac, Lucie. *Outwitting the Gestapo* (University of Nebraska Press, USA, 1993)

Bailey, Rosemary. *Love and War in the Pyrenees* (Phoenix, London, 2009)

Barber, Noel. *The Week France Fell* (Stein & Day, New York, 1976)

Beevor, J. G. *SOE: Recollections and Reflections* (The Bodley Head, London, 1981)

Braddon, Russell. *Nancy Wake, the story of a very brave woman* (Cassell, London, 1956)

Brathwaite, Errol. *Pilot on the Run* (Century Hutchinson NZ Ltd, Auckland, 1986)

Braynard, Frank O. *Picture History of the Normandie* (Dover Pub., New York, 1987)

Brome, Vincent. *The Way Back* (Cassell & Co, London, 1957)

Buckmaster, Maurice. *They Fought Alone* (Odhams Press, Watford, Herts, 1958)

Buckmaster, Maurice. *Specially Employed* (Batchword Press, London, 1952)

Chiaroni, Keren. *The Last of the Human Freedoms* (HarperCollins, New Zealand, 2011)

Cretzmeyer, Stacy. *Your Name is Renée* (Oxford Univ. Press, New York, 1999)

Darling, Donald. *Secret Sunday* (William Kimber, London, 1975)

Diamond, Hanna. *Fleeing Hitler: France 1940* (Oxford Univ. Press, Oxford, 2007)

Eisner, Peter. *The Freedom Line* (HarperCollins Pub, NY, 2004)

Faulks, Sebastian. *Charlotte Grey* (Random House, London, 1998)

Fittko, Lisa. *Escape through the Pyrenees* (Northwestern Univ. Press, Ill, USA, 1991)

Fitzsimons, Peter. *Nancy Wake* (HarperCollins, Sydney, 2001)

Foot, M.R.D *SOE in France* (Her Majesty's Stationery Office, London, 1966)

Gildea, Robert. *Marianne in Chains* (Picador, New York, 2002)

Gold, Mary Jayne. *Crossroads Marseilles 1940* (Doubleday, New York, 1980)

Humbert, Agnes. *Resistance* (Bloomsbury, London, 2009)

Jackson, Julian. *France: The Dark Years 1940-1944* (Oxford Univ. Press, Oxford, 2001)

Kedward, H. R. *Resistance in Vichy France* (Oxford Univ. Press, Oxford, 1978)

Kedward, H R & Wood, Nancy. *The Liberation of France* (Berg Publishers, Oxford, 1995)

Kohner, Hanna and Walter. *Hanna and Walter* (Random House, New York, 1984)

Lavender, Emerson & Sheffe, Norman. *The Evaders* (McGraw-Hill, Ontario, Canada 1992)

Long, Helen. *Safe Houses are Dangerous* (Abson Books, Bristol, England 1989)

Manne, Robert. *The Culture of Forgetting: Helen Demidenko and the Holocaust* (Text Pub. Co., Melbourne, 1996)

Marino, Andy. *A Quiet American* (St. Martin's Griffin, New York, 1999)

Marnham, Patrick. *Resistance and Betrayal* (Random House, New York, 2000)

Maxtone-Graham, John. *Liners to the Sun* (Macmillan Publishing, NY, 1985)

Morhange-Bégué, Claude. *Chamberet* (The Marlboro Press, Vermont, USA, 1987)

Mountfield, David. *The Partisans* (Hamlyn, England, 1979)

Némirovsky, Irene. *Suite Française* (Vintage, New York, 2007)

Nichol, John & Rennell, Tony. *Home Run* (Penguin, London, 2007)

Ottis, Sherri. *Silent Heroes: Downed Airmen and the French Underground* (University Press of Kentucky, Lexington, 2001)

Ousby, Ian. *Occupation* (Cooper Square Press, New York, 2000)

Pryce-Jones, David. *Paris in the 3rd Reich* (William Collins, London, 1981)

Routledge, Paul. *Public Servant, Secret Agent* (Fourth Estate, London, 2002)

Say, Rosemary & Holland, Noel. *Rosie's War* (Michael O'Mara Books, London, 2011)

Vail, Margaret. *Yours is the Earth* (J.B Lippincott Co., New York, 1944)

Vinen, Richard. *The Unfree French: Life under the Occupation* (Yale University Press, USA, 2006)

Wake, Nancy. *The White Mouse* (Pan MacMillan, Australia, 1996)

Walters, Anne-Marie. *Moondrop to Gascony* (Pan books, London, 1955)

Watt, George. *The Comet Connection* University Press of Kentucky, USA, 1990)

Jenny Harrison lives on the North Shore of Auckland, New Zealand with her husband, Howard, and a cat called Scrap. They have four children.

Non-fiction titles:
Debbie's Story
A New Life in New Zealand
To the Child Unborn
The Lives of Alice Pothron

She is also responsible for four novels in the Panui Series – stories as individual as the people who live in the small, entirely fictitious, New Zealand town.
Accidental Hero
The Indigo Kid
The Falling of Shadows
Rusty & Slasher's Guide to Crime

You can buy these titles online at
www.amazon.com,
www.smashwords.com
 www.jennyharrison.co.nz
www.ThePanuiSeries,com,
www.letsbuybooks.weebly.com where you'll find other high-caliber New Zealand authors.